When Relationships Hurt:

52 WAYS TO HEAL

Charlene Sears-Tolbert, M.A.

Order this book online at www.trafford.com
or email orders@trafford.com

Most Trafford titles are also available at major online book retailers.

Print information available on the last page.

ISBN: 978-1-4120-6395-1 (sc)

Trafford rev. 09/19/2018

Trafford
PUBLISHING® www.trafford.com

North America & international
toll-free: 1 888 232 4444 (USA & Canada)
fax: 812 355 4082

Acknowledgement/Dedication

To God, my AM that I AM, my all that I need you to be…if I had
ten-thousand tongues, I could not thank you enough, so I simply say Hallelujah!

To my gift from God, my son Shaka Yohance …loving you keeps me moving
towards the light. Thank you for dancing.

To my "gwanbabee," Jordan Dominique…you bring the sunshine!
P.S. "Who loves you?"

To you, the person holding this book, don't give up before
the miracle happens!

Contents

When Relationships Hurt

Introduction

There is no emotional pain greater than that which comes at the end of a relationship. It doesn't matter what your sexual identity, your race, your occupation, or your religious beliefs the pain of a broken relationship can be devastating. When we lose someone to death the emotional grief is more excusable and acceptable than the grief we feel when a relationship ends. It is acceptable in society to openly grieve the death a loved one, however when our relationships end there is only cursory attention given to our pain. In fact, most people are uncomfortable with the expression of this type of pain and even the most concerned love ones encourage us to 'get over it.'

Most experts agree that it could take one to three years to heal completely from the loss of a significant relationship. No, this does not mean that you can expect to be miserable for one to three years. You can go through your healing process while actively enjoying life. However, after only a few weeks we may begin to feel it is no longer acceptable to bemoan our loss, so we stifle our feelings, put a smile on our face, and try to move on. We try to avoid the pain. Rather than moving through the pain and healing the hurt we may try to bury our feelings in a number of ways. However, whenever something is buried that is not dead, it will come back to haunt us. We find that our feelings continue to surface at the most inconvenient or inopportune times. Quite often, we take these unresolved feelings into our next relationship thereby setting it up for failure, which creates a vicious cycle of pain. The healing process requires that we acknowledge the pain and move through the hurt. The purpose of this book is to support your healing process and to help you let go of the pain when relationships hurt!!

One of the reasons the pain of relationships is so great is because many of us stay in relationships long past the expiration date. The pain of holding on seems easier than the fear of letting go. We agonize, we obsess, and when we finally let go, the relationship has claw marks all over it. Trust me I understand for I too have been there.

I was acutely aware of the claw marks I was leaving behind, the day I divorced for the *second* time the man I married *twice*. Not only did I clearly understand holding on past the expiration date, I also understood the meaning of returning to, and refunding my misery.

On that sunny morning in early spring, I'd gone to the courthouse alone. Separated for fourteen months, I'd convinced myself that this day would be a breeze, easy like a Sunday morning or the warm spring weather we were experiencing. All the friends and family that gathered around me for support at the initial onset of the separation assumed I was okay and had long since returned to the daily routine of their lives. I minimized the emotions I experienced so even those closest to me only gave perfunctory attention to the fact that I was going to divorce the same man twice.

So I went alone. He didn't show up. He couldn't show up. As a result of his gambling addiction he was incarcerated awaiting sentencing on charges brought against him since our separation. I was alone...alone with the hurt and disappointment, because surely the second marriage was supposed to work. I felt shame, humiliation, and loneliness so severe it felt eternal.

My divorce was granted. I asked to have my maiden name restored and the judge granted my request. As I walked out the courtroom, I realized that I felt no connection to my maiden name since I'd used my marriage name for nearly twenty years. My entire professional life was tied to that name—my degrees, my certifications, my mortgage, my bank accounts, my business cards. I chose to obsess over the name issue rather than the fact that I'd just divorce the same man twice. This allowed me to return to work, go through an audit by the state licensing entity, facilitate a group, teach a class, meet a friend for sushi (where I lamented more on the inconvenience of changing my last name), came home, prepared dinner for my son, helped him with his homework, and finally to my pillow where I collapsed from exhaustion. No tears. No emotion. Just exhaustion.

Over the next few days and weeks the emotions began to surface throughout the day like wisps of smoke that quickly evaporated. I did not want to feel the hurt, I wanted to be angry and blame him for messing up my life. I wanted to point the finger at him and make him out to be this horrific monster and me his helpless victim. However, in addition to being a counselor, I have been in my own personal growth process for nearly twenty years through spiritual practices, a twelve-step program, counseling, and hundreds of self-help exercises, and my level of personal growth would not support this way of thinking. I did not have the luxury of a trip on a river in Egypt (de-nial).

You see I know that all of our relationships are a reflection of how we feel about ourselves. I know until we heal ourselves we will continue to attract painful, unhealthy relationships. I had to ask myself the questions that I think is imperative to answer if we truly want to heal, "What is it about *me* that attracted this relationship? What is it *I* need to heal?" Think about all the unhealthy and/or painful relationships you have experienced. Not just the intimate relationships, but also the relationships with co-workers, neighbors, or family members. Now, what is the common denominator in all of those relationships? That's right, go ahead and say it...okay I will say it...me! I am the common denominator in all my relationships and you are the common denominator in all of your relationships.

Pointing the finger keeps us stuck in the problem. This book is about the solution. It is a step-by-step guide to help you move from a place of brokenness, a place of anger and disappointment, to a place of joy, peace, and serenity. I share these exercises with you out of a desire to help you heal. This book is about having the ultimate relationship…with yourself! The healing exercises in this book will lead you on a journey of self-discovery where you may meet yourself for the first time, or you may reunite with yourself, or perhaps you will recreate yourself. Whatever the case may be, love the self that you find and celebrate you!!

You may utilize this book in whatever manner you feel comfortable. In order to apply equally to both men and women this book is gender neutral. The significant other you were/are involved with will be referred to as REMY. REMY is an acronym for Relationships Evaluation Mechanism for Your information. Whenever you see the word, REMY you may substitute your significant other's name or you may refer to your significant other as a REMY.

You may work through this book as part of a support group or do it alone. You can do one exercise a week or work the exercises at a pace that is comfortable for you. You may follow the order of the book or if you feel the need for more immediate help in a particular area turn to that exercise and complete it. Your healing process will be as individual as you are. Nothing works the same for everyone. What is important is that you have found this book and you are willing to heal yourself so that you can heal the pain when relationships hurt.

Exercise #1: *Seek the Help of a Professional if Necessary*

While self-help methods are excellent tools to assist in evaluating and dealing with our issues, there may still be a need to seek the help of professionals. In many instances, self-help work is more beneficial when we recognize the need for professional help and seek out the assistance we need.

The following is an alphabetical listing of organizational websites that could assist you in getting professional help as you move through your healing process. I have included phone numbers where available. [DISCLAIMER: Providing this information is a public service, I do not guarantee the reliability of or the quality of the organizations.]

Alcohol or Drug Problem?
> Substance Abuse & Mental Health Services Administration: 1-800-789-2647
> www.findtreatment.samhsa.gov
> Also see listing of 12-Step programs

Being Stalked? www.stalkinghelp.org

Considering a divorce? www.divorcesource.com 610-770-9342

Credit Counseling?
> www.financialrescueservice.com
> www.debtfree.com 1-800-257-7810

Daily Devotions/Meditations?
> Daily Devotions: www.devotions.net
> Hazeldon Daily Meditations: www.hazeldon.org 1-800-257-7810
> Our Daily Bread: www.gospelconnect/rbc/odb

Legal Help?
> American Bar Association: 1-877-437-3337 www.getareferral.com
> www.getting-legal-advice.com

Need a Church? www.netministries.org

Physical Abuse/Domestic Violence?
> National Domestic Violence Hotline: 1-800-799-7233 www.ndvh.org

Professional Counseling?
American Counseling Association: www.counseling.org 1-800-347-6647 (contd)

National Board of Counseling: www.nbcc.org
The American Association of Pastoral Counseling: www.aapc.org
www.1-800-Therapist.com (Counselor referral)

Sexual Abuse? Rape, Abuse, & Incest National Network: www.rainn.org

Single Parent? www.singleparentcentral.com

12-Step Program?
Alcohol www.alcohol-anonymous.org
Al-Anon www.al-anon.org
Co-Dependent www.codependents.org
Cocaine www.ca.org
Debtors www.debtoranonymous.org
Emotions www.emotionsanonymous.org
Gambling www.gamblersanonymous.org
Incest www.siawso.org
Narcotics www.na.org
Nicotine www.nicotine-anonymous.org
Overeating www.overeatersanonymous.org
Sex & Love www.slaafws.org

I will seek the following assistance:

_____

_____

_____

_____

_____

_____

_____

_____

Exercise #2: *Start a Support Group*

A support group is not designed to take the place of professional counseling. If you find that you are having a difficult time dealing with your feelings or you have a difficult time when other people deal with their feelings, you probably could benefit from individual counseling with a professional counselor. However, the therapeutic significance of a support group is invaluable to helping you move through the healing process when relationships hurt.

Starting your support group

- For emotional safety and comfort the support group should be gender specific (women supporting women/ men supporting men).

- Unfortunately, there is not a shortage of people dealing with the hurt of a relationship. Ask family members, friends, neighbors, co-workers, church members, etc. Anyone you know that is divorced, separated, or single could probably benefit from a support group that focuses on healing the hurt from a relationship.

- To establish an intimately supportive environment limit the group to three to six participants.

- If schedules allow it, plan to meet once a week or at the very least meet twice monthly. Meeting on the same day and time (i.e. the second and fourth Tuesday at 7:00 p.m.) creates consistency and makes it easier for all group members.

- The allotted time for the support group averages about sixty minutes. You may want to allow an extra half hour either prior to or afterwards for refreshments, (alcoholic beverages are discouraged as they may impede the therapeutic process). It is suggested to use an alarm clock to start the support group and to remind you when the allotted time is over.

- Plan to meet at a private location such as a participant's home. It is a good idea to rotate the meeting place among each participant's home so as to not place an unfair burden on any one person (this also prevents establishing "ownership" of the group by any one individual).

Suggested Items for Support Group

Your journal
Pens and paper
Post-it-notes
A timer or an alarm clock
A box of tissues

Scented candles
Individual copies of *"52 Ways to Heal When Relationships Hurt."*

Healing music (I recommend Iyanla Vanzant's *"In the meantime the music that tells the story"*). Play the music before and afterwards but is discouraged during the actual group meeting.

I will invite the following people to join my support group:

_____

_____

_____

_____

_____

_____

_____

_____

_____

_____

_____

SUPPORT GROUP
THE 12 COMMITMENTS
(Maybe Read at Each Group Meeting)

This support group is a therapeutic opportunity to heal from the grief and disappointment we find ourselves confronted with when our relationships hurt. In order to ensure a healing and supportive environment we agree to commit to the following:

1. We are committed to making this group a priority in our lives, therefore, we will make every effort to attend all sessions and to be on time.

2. We are committed to absolute confidentiality. We will not share anything shared by another group member outside of our group. This will cultivate emotional safety and group integrity.

3. We are committed to creating a nonjudgmental atmosphere by allowing others to be where they are in their process. We recognize that we are all perfectly imperfect and healing is a process.

4. We are committed to only offering suggestions and not forcing our opinions on others. We avoid using the word "should" when speaking to others or ourselves.

5. We are committed to listening attentively and respecting each member's sharing. We refrain from interrupting while someone is speaking.

6. We are committed to use "I" statements such as 'I feel…" rather than "you are…"

7. We are committed to being respectful of the time and the need for others to share.

8. We are committed to participate in experiential exercises such as journaling, mirror work, role-playing, affirmations, and etc., both in the group and as "homework" assignments as suggested by "*When Relationships Hurt: 52 Ways to Heal*" and as agreed upon by the group.

9. We are committed to sharing inspirational creations (poems, songs, essays, books, etc.) with one another.

10. We are committed to continually improve our spirituality and our reliance on God and to practice prayer, meditation and contemplation, to move beyond our place of pain into all of the goodness life has in store for us.

11. We are committed to nurturing the relationship with ourselves by taking loving care of our bodies and developing emotional, intellectual, social, and financial self-sufficiency.

12. We are committed to sharing the tools of our healing process with others that are seeking healing from their pain when relationships hurt.

SUGGESTED MEETING FORMAT

o   The person hosting the group in their home may facilitate the group.

o   Begin with a moment of quiet meditation followed by a short prayer. (The short version of the Serenity Prayer {See below} is always appropriate)

o   Thank the group members for coming out to support the group.

o   Handle any housekeeping issues at this time. Ask that all cell phones be in the silent mode.

o   Ask the group members to read (round robin style) the twelve commitments. (Each member should be given a copy of the twelve commitments at the first meeting)

o   At the first meeting have each member introduce him or herself and describe why they have decided to join this group (about five minutes). Otherwise, allow each member five to ten minutes to check-in and share his or her process, progress, or regression since the last meeting. You may want to use the timer to keep everyone mindful of the time. (Always check in and ask if anyone is having a particular hard time at the moment and need to share right away).

o   Review the group exercise/activity with the group members.

o   Complete group exercise/activity.

o   Allow twenty to thirty minutes to share any feelings the exercise/activity may bring up.

o   Discuss any homework or reading assignments for next group.

o   Re-confirm the next meeting date, time, and location.

o   Check-in with all group members to ensure everyone is okay to end the group.

o   Close by joining hands and saying the Serenity Prayer (if chosen prayer).

Serenity Prayer by Reinhold Niebur

God, Grant me the Serenity to accept the things I cannot change
The Courage to change the things I can, and
The Wisdom to know the difference

Exercise #3: *Develop a Support System*

At no other time in your life will a support system be more important than healing from the emotional trauma when relationships hurt. When relationships hurt, we need the help of supportive individuals to help us heal. A healthy support system provides the following:

- Someone that has an empathetic understanding of what you are going through. Those who themselves may have experience the pain when relationships hurt and can validate your feelings.

- Someone you can honestly share with without feeling judged.

- Someone who can provide sound counsel or advice—maybe a professional counselor or a mentor. This should be someone whose opinion you respect.

- Someone that will cry with you

- Someone that will laugh with you

- Someone that will help you be accountable to your commitments and responsibilities.

- Someone that you can simply hangout with and go to a movie, dinner, or other social activity.

- Someone that provides spiritual support, maybe a prayer partner

- Someone that encourages and motivates you to be your best.

- Someone with similar interest/hobbies.

It is unfair to expect anyone person to fill all of our needs. Our support system should include at least five people who may have more than one role. We should also be willing to provide support to others as well.

Name at least five supportive people that could make up your support system. It is okay if you don't currently have five people in your support system. I strongly urge you to start your own support group as described in the <u>Starting Your Own Support Group</u> section of this book.

Use the following diagram to see how well rounded your support system is. Again, it is okay if you find areas lacking, you can work on filling those areas.

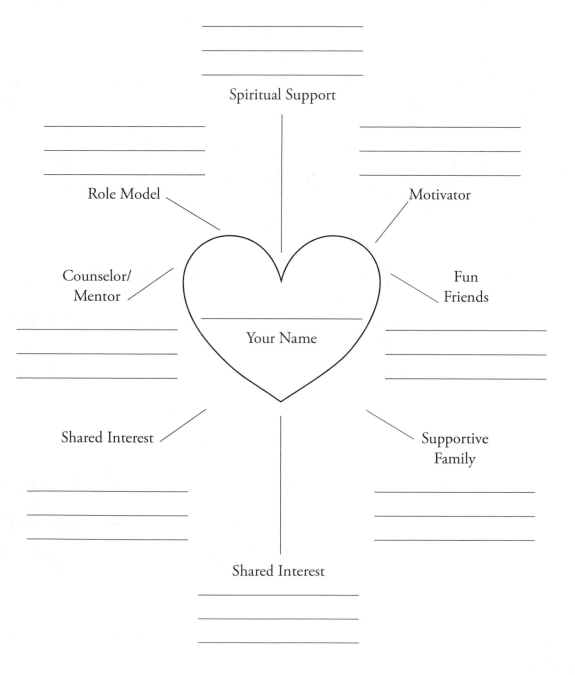

Exercise #4: *Journaling/Feeling Log*

Journaling is one of the key and primary tools we use to deal with feelings when relationships hurt. As you began your journey towards healing, understand this:

- Feelings are not facts!
- Feelings are not bad or good!
- Feelings are not right or wrong!
- Feelings are just feelings nothing more nothing less!

We often place a lot of judgment on our feelings, but the truth is it is not the *feelings* that create the problems. It is what we *do* with the feelings that cause the problem. Therefore, it is imperative that we learn how to <u>process</u> our feelings and not always <u>act</u> on them. We often give our feelings far too much power and we mistakenly believe that if we feel something it must true. We need to learn how to have our feelings without judgment and realize just because we *feel* something does not make it a reality.

Writing your thoughts/feelings on a regular basis can be very healing for a number of reasons.

1) It gives you the opportunity to vent and release pent up emotions.
2) Feelings and emotions seem more manageable on paper than inside our head.
3) It is a form of self-discovery.
4) It boost your self-esteem and self-value when your take time to do something for yourself.
5) It provides an opportunity to take an objective look at what you are feeling.
6) It allows you to observe your healing process.

Journaling can take any form that feels comfortable. The most important thing is that you ***write!!!*** You can use your journal to do all of your written healing exercise. You can write letters to yourself, letter to God, or letters to your REMY[1]. You can begin each entry with, "Today I feel…or Dear Diary…" How you use your journal is up to you. There is no write (pun intended) or wrong way.

Make a commitment to journal, be as specific as possible, which days, what time of day, and how many minutes will you obligate to for this purpose. This will help you hold yourself accountable. If you miss a day or two, don't beat yourself up, journal about it and move on.

I, _____, make a commitment to journal for at least _____ minutes at least _____ times a week. The best time of day for me to journal is _____. Share this commitment with someone that can help hold you accountable.

---

[1]<u>R</u>elationship <u>E</u>valuation <u>M</u>echanism for <u>Y</u>our Information, or the person you were/are in a relationship with.

The following is a list of feeling words that may help you identify your feelings:

Abandoned	Delighted	Guilty	Outraged
Adamant	Despairing	Happy	Overwhelmed
Angry	Disappointed	Helpless	Peaceful
Annoyed	Distracted	Honored	Rejected
Anxious	Distraught	Hurt	Relieved
Awed	Disturbed	Ignored	Sad
Betrayed	Eager	Impressed	Satisfied
Bitter	Ecstatic	Infatuated	Scared
Blissful	Embarrassed	Inspired	Shocked
Bored	Energetic	Intimidated	Skeptical
Burdened	Envious	Isolated	Startled
Calm	Exasperated	Irritated	Tense
Cheated	Fearful	Jealous	Terrified
Cheerful	Flustered	Joyous	Trapped
Combative	Frantic	Kind	Troubled
Condemned	Frustrated	Lonely	Uneasy
Confused	Free	Loving	Vulnerable
Content	Furious	Lustful	Wonderful
Crushed	Glad	Miserable	Worried
Defeated	Grateful	Nervous	Zealous

Using the following guide journal your feelings for the next seven days. Include as many of the feeling words as possible. Continue to journal throughout your healing process, and it will probably become a life-long habit.

Today I feel:

_____

_____

_____

_____

_____

_____

_____

I think it is coming from:

_____

_____

_____

_____

_____

_____

The best thing I can do about this is:

_____

_____

_____

_____

_____

_____

Today I am grateful because:

_____

_____

_____

_____

_____

_____

Exercise #5: REMY! *Pad*

- Your REMY pad should be a small spiral notebook that fits easily in your purse, brief case, jacket pocket, or glove compartment.

- Its primary purpose is to serve as a portable journal and should always be easily accessible.

- Use your REMY pad to write all thoughts that you have of your REMY throughout the day.

- This is an excellent tool for releasing your emotions rather than keeping them pent up inside or acting on them.

- If you are feeling the urge to call or make contact with your REMY write your thoughts in the REMY pad instead, and call someone from your support system and share your feelings.

- Write whatever comes to mind without judgment.

- Do not filter your thoughts. You can always rip out the sheet of paper and shred it or burn it. Writing the thoughts exactly as they come into your mind helps to release the emotions and facilitate healing when relationships hurt.

Remember...

- Write your thoughts without judgment.

- Feelings are not necessarily fact! Just because you *feel* something does not make it so.

- You do not *have* to act on your feelings.

- Write them down.

- Share them with a supportive person

Often we try to resist the thoughts and feelings of our REMY, however, what we resist persist. Have the thoughts, have the feelings. Allow them to come up and out of you. Over the next week, write every thought of your REMY that comes to mind. Write without judgment and write whatever comes to mind without censoring your thoughts. Remember to use paper that is disposable so that you may destroy it later if you like.

Continue to use your REMY pad as you move through the healing process.

---

¹Relationship Evaluation Mechanism for Your Information, or the person you were/are in a relationship with.

Exercise #6: *Trust in the Process*

As I was writing this book, I was returning home to Orlando on a flight from Detroit. The plane ride was incredibly turbulent. As a matter of fact, in all my years of flying and the hundreds of plane rides I have experienced I cannot ever remember a more tumultuous ride. It was feeling very scary as though I was at the top of a roller coaster waiting for the drop and I was starting to sweat. The pilot came over the intercom system and in what I am sure was a, practiced to appear calm voice said, "I apologize for the extremely turbulent ride, however there is no altitude we can rise to in order to avoid the turbulence. Unfortunately, we are going to have to ride this one out."

This I thought is the perfect example of powerlessness. I had no power over the plane, the clouds, or the weather…I had to trust the process. When relationships hurt unfortunately, we just may have to ride it out. Sometimes there is no way around our hurt, no way over our pain, sometimes the only way out is through it.

As I held onto my seat to keep from being bounced around the plane and struggled to keep my lunch down, I looked around the plane and saw my fellow travelers in distress as well. I was not alone. We were all uncomfortable, yet we all held on. Despite the discomfiture, no one was trying to get off the plane. No one said, "Stop the plane I want to get off." Of course, we all realize how insane that would be; yet many times we are unable to trust the process in our lives. We end up aborting the healing process in mid-flight and causing ourselves more pain.

We have to learn to trust the process. There is no feeling that will last forever. Feelings are transient and they are constantly changing. What you felt last week, last month, or certainly, last year, you probably do not feel to the same extreme today. Trust the same about what you are feeling today -- it too shall pass.

If life is anything, it is change. All things change. Nothing remains the same. I once received an email by an unknown author that told a little story. As the story goes, once upon a time a king ruled a vast country. This king called to him the wisest men in all the land. He charged them to go to the four corners of the earth and to seek the counsel of the wisest men on the earth. He promised to bestow riches untold to the one that could bring back one seed of truth… one saying…one sentence by which he could live his life. A sentence that he could keep forever in view, and which should be true and appropriate in all times and situations.. After several years, the wise men returned from their journeys and came before the king. The first three came before him in sorrow with their heads bowed. With much grief, they explained to the king that they were unable to find just one seed of truth that would ring true in all situations. Finally, the fourth wise man appeared before the king. He stated, "My king after many years and much searching throughout the world, I have brought back to you the one seed of truth that you may apply to any and all situations. Be it a tragedy or a joy, whether you are happy or sad the one truth that will always remain the same is, "This Too Shall Pass." No matter what you are going through right now…this too shall pass. No matter what it feels like…this too shall pass. Whether you are happy or you are sad, this too shall pass.

Describe a time from your experiences when you felt emotional pain:

_____

_____

_____

_____

_____

_____

Think about how you felt about that situation at the time.

How do you feel about it today? What has changed?

_____

_____

_____

_____

_____

_____

How can you use this experience to help you trust the process in your situation today?

_____

_____

_____

_____

_____

Exercise #7: *A Personal Relationship*

Do you feel a personal connection to God? Do you feel you have a personal and intimate relationship with God? Few of us have been taught true "relationship" with God, but rather our beliefs are based in ritualistic dogma. Many of us developed our belief system about God based on fear-based theology. However, if we are to heal our hurts and move from a place of despair to a place of hope it is important that we began to develop a healthy belief system based on the belief of a loving, caring and forgiving God that has the power to get us through any obstacle we may face in life. It is important that we develop a personal understanding of God, which comes through developing a personal, "relationship," with Him.

The root word of relationship is relă or "to connect." Think about a relay race where the runners connect to pass the baton or take the baton with a common goal in mind. So in this sense the root word implies to give and take. However, most of us do not experience this give and take in our understanding of God. Rather our discourse with God often consists of one-sided discourse where we might "pray" or 'talk" to God. We ask God to do things for us and to protect our love ones. We ask God to give us things, to keep us safe, very simply put we make requests. The more conscious of us may also give thanks, but the dialogue is really a monologue because it is one-sided. Communication is a two-way street and in order to have relationship there must be communication on both sides.

Imagine going out on a first date at a very elegant restaurant and as you sat across the table from your potential partner the conversation sounded something like this. "I like these flowers, but my favorite flower is orchid, especially the color purple. Oh, did you see that movie? It's one of my favorite movies. I can't imagine living like that though. I don't like rural living…I prefer the city. But my favorite is the islands. Oh, I love the beach and the ocean. I would love for you to take me to Aruba or maybe we can go on a Western Caribbean cruise sometime. Those are the best. And the food is great. I love exotic foods. Maybe the next time we have dinner you can take me to this great Thai food restaurant I heard about. And there is this new Creole restaurant I want you to take me to, because I love Creole food. You must take me to Mardi Gras next year and eat the authentic foods of New Orleans. I love the boutiques in New Orleans and blah, blah, blah. What do you think your dinner partner is thinking by this time? Probably, trying to figure out how to get as far away as possible.

We all can see how one-sided this conversation is, but the reality is that this is how most of us talk to God. We have a litany of requests and concerns. We go on and on making ourselves known to God, but how interested are we in getting to know who God is? How much time do we spend listening to God? If God spoke to us, would we even recognize His voice? How often do we ask God what we can do for Him? Do we know what God likes, what displeases God? How much time do we spend getting to know God? It is through developing and maintaining a close personal relationship with God that we are able to trust the healing process.

Imagine that you could write a want ad for God. Imagine if God could be anything you want Him or Her to be; possessing any qualities and powers that you desire, what would your want ad look like. Take a few minutes, think about that, and in the following space write your own personal want ad for God. Some things to think about are: How do you relate to God. What is it you need from God? What are you willing to give God? Be creative and make it fun (the following are some examples of want ads).

Wanted	Wanted
Male/Female God with experience in healing the broken heart. Must be loving, gentle, and dependable and available twenty-four-seven. Must have all the answers, love to solve problems and guide me in the right direction. Good communication and listening skills are a must.	Omnipotent, omniscient, and omnipresent God to develop a loving life-long relationship. Need to be able to carry me through the bad times and walk with me through the rest. The hours are long, there is no vacation or time off. I will pay you through my praise, devotion, and service to others.

WANTED

_____

_____

_____

_____

_____

_____

Review your want ad in comparison with what you believe about God. Is there any need that you listed that you feel God cannot meet? The reality is God can be whatever you need Him to be. It is God's desire to have relationships with us. Remember what we think is best for us is not always the best thing for us. Sometimes God is moving things out of our way to create room for something new. Repeat your want ad aloud three times a day for the next seven days.

Exercise #8: *Looking for Love in All the Right Places*

Grieving our relationships is often accompanied by a sense of lost love. We think we are not being loved or there isn't enough love, we may even think we will never be loved again. We associate love to "that feeling" we may have or had towards our REMY. The truth is love is not an emotion but rather the manifestation of the essence of God. God is Love and this Love is manifested all around you, everywhere! The problem is we have been looking for Love in all the wrong places.

Now that you have a better understanding of what it is you want in a relationship with God, it is important that you begin to develop your personal understanding of Him through recognizing the ways He communicates with you. How do you know God is talking to you? God is omnipresent (everywhere—all the time). Begin to pay attention to the many ways God speaks to you throughout the day. Remember there has been only one recording of a burning bush, but God continues to speak.

There is a little story about a very religious man. This man lived in a town where a flood was coming. As the story goes, an evacuation team went to the man's home to warn him of the need to evacuate. The team offered to transport the man to safer ground. The man refused to leave his home declaring his unfailing belief in the power of God to save him. The religious man went on to accuse everyone that was evacuating as being faithless. He felt righteous in his belief in God to save him and spent his time praying for God to save him from the flood. The flood came and as the waters begin to rise inside of his home, a team of rescuers came by in a boat and asked the religious man to get aboard so that he could be brought to safety. Again, the man refused and stated God would save him. The waters continued to rise. Finally, the waters were so high the man moved to his rooftop, where he prayed vigilantly for God to save him. A helicopter flew over and seeing the man praying they let down the rope ladder and shouted for the man to climb up into the safety of the helicopter. Again, the man refused and shouted back he believed in the power of God to save him. Well the floods continued and the man drowned. He went to heaven and he went before God, but he was very distraught. The man said to God, "I am a very religious man, I prayed to you religiously and I believed that you would save me. I do not understand why you let me drown." God simply answered, "Look, I sent you an evacuation team, a boat, and a helicopter, what more did you want?"

While we can see the humor in this story, how often do we miss God because we are looking in all the wrong places? When was the last time God spoke to you? Imagine spending your days looking for God's Love and truly communicating with God. Have you ever seen a butterfly take flight? What about biting into a sweet and juicy peach? Have you ever been stuck in a traffic jam and suddenly notice the bright orange of a setting sun? Those are all examples of God's Love expressing itself. Spend the next seven days looking for God's Love in all things and record them. Look for at least 52 ways, which may seem like a lot right now, but once you get use to looking for God's Love, you will be surprised by how much love there really is in the world.

1. _____

2. _____

3. _____

4. _____

5. _____

6. _____

7. _____

8. _____

9. _____

10. _____

11. _____

12. _____

13. _____

14. _____

15. _____

16. _____

17. _____

18. _____

19. _____

20. _____

21. _____

22. _____

23. _____

24. _____

25. _____

26. _____

27. _____

28. _____

29. _____

30. _____

31. _____

32. _____

33. _____

34. _____

35. _____

36. _____

37. _____

38. _____

39. _____

40. _____

41. _____

42. _____

43. _____

44. _____

45. _____

46. _____

47. _____

48. _____

49. _____

50. _____

51. _____

52. _____

After completing the, "Looking for Love," exercise, has your understanding of whom God is changed in anyway? If so, how?

_____

_____

_____

_____

_____

   Now that you are developing a personal relationship with God, what are you willing to do to maintain the relationship? Some examples maybe attending religious services, participate in a 12-step program, reading daily devotions, studying spiritual or religious books, prayer, meditation, study groups, spending time in nature, etc.

I am willing to commit to the following to improve my relationship with God:

_____

_____

_____

_____

_____

_____

_____

_____

_____

_____

_____

Exercise #9: *52 Ways to Practice Spiritual Principles*

The Spirit is the eternal part of us that connects us to the oneness of life. It is the place of highest truth and intelligence. Our spirit connects us to the all-knowing, all-powerful, ever-present love of God. It is this omniscient, omnipotent, omnipresent love that is the source for all of our needs and the basis for our healing when relationships hurt.

Spirituality is practicing love-based principles that connect us to God. These spiritual principles are our weapons in the warfare to win back our hearts. If these principles governed all of our actions and thoughts, we would lead a peace-filled life free from fear and doubt.

52 spiritual principles that we want to practice in our daily lives are:

Acceptance	Endurance	Justice	Purpose
Appreciation	Enthusiasm	Kindness	Reverence
Authenticity	Fairness	Laughter	Self-Acceptance
Bravery	Faith	Loyalty	Self-Discipline
Commitment	Forgiveness	Motivation	Selflessness
Compassion	Generosity	Obedience	Service
Consideration	Gentleness	Open-Minded	Sharing
Courage	Gratitude	Optimism	Surrender
Courteousness	Helpfulness	Passion	Tolerance
Dedication	Honesty	Patience	Trust
Determination	Hope	Perseverance	Truth
Discernment	Humility	Praise	Unity
Empathy	Integrity	Prayerfulness	Willingness

All of these principles are manifestations of Love. It is said the best way to get what we want is to become what we want. If we want love, we should practice being loving by embodying the above spiritual principles. The following seven principles are indispensable to helping us heal when relationships hurt. Make a concentrated effort to practice one of the seven principles over the next seven days. The definition that I give for each principle is my description of how we can use the principle to help us heal when relationships hurt.

Day One—Willingness

Willingness is an internal commitment or decision to do something because we understand it needs doing. Not to be confused with readiness. We may not be ready to do a healing exercise, but we have the willingness to do it anyway. If I waited until I was ready to get up out of my comfortable bed, I would probably stay there all day. However, I get up because I have a willingness, which moves me into action. You may not be "ready" to let go of a relationship; however are you, "willing" to work towards letting go? Essentially willingness is based upon the commitment to do something rather than the "feelings." When we do not "feel" like accomplishing a task, willingness will move us forward.

Today I will/have practiced willingness by

_____

_____

_____

_____

_____

_____

_____

I can continue to use willingness to help me heal in the following ways:

_____

_____

_____

_____

_____

_____

_____

Day Two—Faith

Faith is the belief that things will get better. It allows us to get through the roughest storm, the darkest night, and the deepest valley because we know in that place of knowing that this too shall pass and I can make it through the day. Faith is not based on the situation we currently feel but the belief in the possibility of something better. When we are hurting or consumed with doubt it is faith the helps us make it to our pillow at night, and gives us strength to face another day. We cannot see the light at the end of the tunnel, but faith tells us if we keep putting one foot in front of the other, eventually we will see that light.

Today I will/have practiced faith by

_____

_____

_____

_____

_____

_____

_____

I can continue to use faith to help me heal in the following ways:

_____

_____

_____

_____

_____

_____

_____

Day Three—Courage

Courage is not lack of fear, but rather it is the ability to feel the fear and still confront the situation. As we move through the healing process there will be many days we may be paralyzed by our fears. The spiritual principle of courage allows us to move forward and do what we need to do regardless of our fears. The willingness to heal from the hurt of your relationship requires courage. You are embarking on a journey with uncharted territory and although there may be some fear associated with it, courage moves us into right action.

Today I will/have practiced courage by

_____

_____

_____

_____

_____

_____

I can continue to use courage to help me heal in the following ways:

_____

_____

_____

_____

_____

_____

_____

Day Four—Self-Discipline

Self-discipline is our ability to moderate or control our own behaviors. We often have a hard time giving ourselves a no. Most often, we want what we want when we want it, and we want it now. Not all that we want is best for us. We can use self-discipline to enforce boundaries we have set for ourselves. Self-discipline allows us to keep the commitments we have made to ourselves so we may do the work required to heal when relationships hurt.

Today I will/have practiced self-discipline by

_____

_____

_____

_____

_____

_____

I can continue to use self-discipline to help me heal in the following ways:

_____

_____

_____

_____

_____

_____

_____

Day Five—Acceptance

Acceptance is a choice to deal with situations just as they are, rather than how we wish them to be. We may not like what is going on or we may not agree with what is happening, but it is important that we accept the fact that it is so. Acceptance is the ability to recognize and receive the truth with an open mind. When we are hurting, there is a tendency to want to deny our reality in order to ease the pain. Of course, this only prolongs the process and does not change the reality. With acceptance, we can deal with a thing exactly as it is and not as we want it to be.

Today I will/have practiced acceptance by

_____

_____

_____

_____

_____

_____

_____

I can continue to use acceptance to help me heal in the following ways:

_____

_____

_____

_____

_____

_____

_____

Day Six—Honesty

Honesty is the ability to honor our true authentic selves. To acknowledge truthfully, who we are, what we feel, and what we think. Because of our own judgments or because we may fear the judgments of others there maybe times when we are hesitant about sharing our true feelings or thoughts. However, our healing process requires complete honesty with ourselves as well as others. I believe that we cannot move from a place we are not. If we are planning a trip to California from Florida, but we are pretending to be in New York we will never get where we are trying to go. Emotionally, we must acknowledge exactly where we are so that we may get to where we are trying to go.

Today I will/have practiced honesty by

_____

_____

_____

_____

_____

_____

_____

I can continue to use honesty to help me heal in the following ways:

_____

_____

_____

_____

_____

_____

_____

Day Seven—Discernment

Discernment is the ability to hear without hearing, to see without seeing, and to knowing without knowing. It is the practice of listening to our inner voice and to trust its guidance. Discernment may be the feeling we get in our gut about a situation or we may refer to it as intuition. Our spirit is connected to God who has all knowledge about all things. God is always guiding us into right action, but we must practice discerning the voice of our spirit.

Today I will/have practiced discernment by

_____

_____

_____

_____

_____

_____

_____

I can continue to use discernment to help me heal in the following ways:

_____

_____

_____

_____

_____

_____

_____

Exercise #10: *Maintaining the Connection*

Visualize a beautiful floor lamp. An eclectic blend of ceramic, steel, and glass with intricate carvings comprises the entire length of the base. The lampshade is made from beautiful raw silk and crystal beads. It is a beautiful piece of furniture. However, the lamp is not plugged into an electrical outlet, so despite its stunning beauty it is not fulfilling its full purpose. When it is connected to the power source, it can then shine brightly in its true purpose. This analogy applies to human condition as well. We must maintain the connection to our power source if we are to walk in our true purpose.

It is important as we move through our healing process that we consciously devote time each and everyday to nurturing our inner spirit. Exactly how you do this will be as individual as you are. It is not as important what you do, as long as you do something. Devoting quality time to nurture your inner spirit has many benefits. It improves your sense of self-worth, self-value, and self-esteem. It prepares you and helps you to cope with the stress of daily living. In addition, becoming centered in devotion will bring balance in your life when dealing with the pain when relationships hurt.

Make a commitment to devote some time each day.

- What time would be most convenient for you? Be consistent with the time. I am committed to spend time in devotion everyday at _____ am/pm.
- How much time are you willing to spend? I am committed to spending _____ minutes in devotion everyday.
- Devote a special place for your devotion time. (Your bedroom, the kitchen table, the sun porch, under your favorite tree, etc.) The place I will designate for my devotional time is _____
- I commit to practicing the following during my devotion time:
  ____ Prayer
  ____ Meditation
  ____ Quiet contemplation
  ____ Journaling
  ____ Listening to positive uplifting music
  ____ Being in nature
  ____ Journaling
  ____ Reading daily devotions, spiritual books
  ____ Healing Exercises
  ____ Other _____
  ____ Other _____
  ____ Other _____

Commitment   Commitment   Commitment   Commitment

I've been told that if you do a thing twenty-one times it becomes a habit. Make a commitment for the next twenty-one days to practice your devotion. Keep a journal of what you do each day. If you miss a day that is okay—you can always re-commitment!

Day 1 _____

Day 2 _____

Day 3 _____

Day 4 _____

Day 5 _____

Day 6 _____

Day 7 _____

Day 8 _____

Day 9 _____

Day 10 _____

Day 11 _____

Day 12 _____

Day 13 _____

Day 14 _____

Day 15 _____

Day 16 _____

Day 17 _____

Day 18 _____

Day 19 _____

Day 20 _____

Day 21 _____

Exercise #11: *When Relationships Hurt*
Free Form Writing

Free form writing is a therapeutic way to quickly sort through the thoughts in our mind and vent pent up emotions. In this exercise, you write continuously for a set amount of time <u>all</u> thoughts that come to your mind no matter how irrational or odd the thoughts may seem. Free form writing is an excellent exercise to help heal the pain when relationships hurt because it allows you to move past the surface thoughts on your mind and vent your emotions and feelings. Some guidelines for free form writing are as follows:

- Decide how long you are going to write, five to ten minutes is usually sufficient. Use a timer to alert you when the allotted time is up. This is important because once you start writing it is easy to lose track of the time.

- Once you start writing, continue to write no matter what comes to your mind. It may seem strange (Popeye has big arms) or off the subject, (I wonder if the tuna salad is still fresh). Write it down and just keep writing no matter how odd or irrational the thoughts may seem.

- Do not filter your thoughts so that they seem appropriate.

- Don't censor your language. Whatever comes up let it come out.

- Do not try to correct your grammar or spelling—it doesn't matter —just keep writing.

- Don't think about what you are writing—just write!

The first set of free form writing exercises are dealing with your REMY[1]. If you are in a support group you may do this exercise in your group or as a homework assignment and share it with your group. Or, it is perfectly okay to do the exercise alone as well. Wherever or however you choose to do this exercise, it is important that you do not change or edit what you wrote when you are done. Remember, the first thoughts that come to your minds are very important and can give you a lot of insight into yourself.

For each phrase, spend three to five minutes responding in free form style

(1) What I miss the most about _____ is

_____

_____

_____

_____

_____

_____

_____

_____

_____

(2) The healthiest way I can fill this void is

_____

_____

_____

_____

_____

_____

_____

_____

_____

_____

(3) What hurts the most when I think about _____ is

_____

_____

_____

_____

_____

_____

_____

_____

_____

_____

(4) The best thing I can do for myself to feel better is

_____

_____

_____

_____

_____

_____

_____

_____

_____

- Re-read your responses without judgment.

- Think about what you wrote. What does it mean to you?

- Write about any feelings/reactions you have in your journal.

- Every couple of days for the next week, re-visit your response and journal your feelings. As time goes by, does your reaction to your response seem to change?

- After seven days re-do the exercise answering the same questions in the same allotted time.

(1) What I miss the most about _____ is

_____

_____

_____

_____

_____

_____

_____

_____

_____

(2) The healthiest way I can fill this void is

_____

_____

_____

_____

_____

_____

_____

_____

_____

(3) What hurts the most when I think about _____ is

_____

_____

_____

_____

_____

_____

_____

_____

_____

(4) The best thing I can do for myself to feel better is

_____

_____

_____

_____

_____

_____

_____

_____

_____

Is there any difference in the way you answered the questions? If so, what?

_____

_____

_____

_____

_____

_____

_____

_____

Why do you think this is so?

_____

_____

_____

_____

_____

_____

_____

_____

_____

Exercise #12: *Creating a Collage*
When Relationships Hurt

SUPPLIES NEEDED:

½ Poster board
5 – 10 Magazines
Scissors
Glue stick
Paper glue

Collage work is a very creative therapeutic expression of your emotions when relationships hurt. What do you feel? Are you sad, hurt, or disappointed? Use the collage to bring a visual representation of your inner most feelings.

- It is important while doing your collage not to think too much about the pictures in the beginning. Flip through the magazines and look for pictures or words that express how you are feeling. If you feel an urge to cut it out — cut it out. It could be a plate of spaghetti or a garbage can spilling over. Mine including things I hated most like spiders and snakes, but also include beautiful sandy beaches. It was a combination of my hurt and anger as well as the things I missed about the relationship.
- Cut as many pictures as possible in one sitting. You don't have to use every picture that you cut out, but cutting the pictures out and having them available gives you the option later.
- Paste the pictures to the poster board. You may use the glue stick to attach cutouts temporarily until you make a final decision. Again, there is no right or wrong. This is your creation. Allow your creative energy to flow.
- Once your collage is complete, spend a few minutes sitting quietly and meditating on the pictures.
- Describe what the pictures mean to you now when you think about them in the context of when relationships hurt?

_____

_____

_____

_____

_____

_____

_____

_____

_____

• Is there an emotion that seems to standout more, such as anger or sadness?

_____

_____

_____

Allow yourself to feel the emotion. Cry if you feel like crying, it is okay.
Write about your emotions in free form (without thinking, write as quickly as you can everything you feel)

I feel _____, because

_____

_____

_____

The best thing I can do for myself to help me feel better is:

_____

_____

_____

_____

_____

If you are comfortable with the idea, leave your collage in a visible place for five to seven days. Continue to journal daily any feelings/reactions the collage evokes. After seven days sit quietly with the collage and again reflect on the pictures.

❖   Are the feelings as strong?

❖   Is there another emotion that feels stronger?

❖   Has the intensity decreased?

If you like, please feel free to share your collage with your group or someone in your support system.

Exercise #13: Affirmations: *The Power of the Spoken Word*

"Sticks and stones may break my bones but words shall surely kill me."

There is life and death in the tongue. The spoken word is so extremely powerful that I would venture to say that it is the most powerful tool of creation we have. It is my belief that everything on this planet came into existence because of the creative force of the spoken word. Yet we often do not pay attention to the words we say to others, or even more importantly the words we use to speak to ourselves.

Who we are today is a result of words that people have spoken over us, and words we have internalized and then spoken to ourselves. We are all born with a clean slate—we have no judgments, no guilt, and no shame. As a matter of fact, we have no frame of reference for any negative emotions or thoughts about ourselves, or our situation in life. Have you ever seen babies playing with themselves? They are absolutely in love with themselves. The have no judgments. Then someone *says* 'your legs are too skinny,' 'your hair is too curly," "your skin is too dark," "you cry too much". Even more damaging are statements like, "you are stupid," "you will never amount to anything," "you always make a mess" or "you make me sick." We then began to form opinions about ourselves based on other people judgments and the words they have spoken to us. We internalize those words and they become our truth. Two words that are extremely limiting and damaging to our self-esteem are *should* and *can't*.

Imagine as a child, you were told over and over how much you were loved and that you were absolutely perfect. You were constantly reminded that you deserved the best, and you could do or become anything you wanted. Continuously you were told how intelligent and creative you were and that it was a joy to be in your presence. How different would your life be today if you had grown up with these positive words as your truth? In reality, most of us did not grow up hearing life affirming words, but rather we heard negative words. We internalized these negative words and they became our truth. Well, the good news is it is not too late. You can use positive affirming words to re-create the messages we send to ourselves.

We constantly re-affirm our lives with negative messages like "I am always late," or "There is never enough money," or "I could never do that." We say things like "I am always sick," and then wonder why we are always sick. Instead try saying, "I am healthy and whole," even if you are in bed with the flu—you will speed up your healing and send your immune system a message. Instead of saying, "there is never enough," repeatedly affirm, "all my needs are always met," or "I flow through life easy and effortlessly."

- Affirmations use the creative energy of words to call those things that are not into existence.

- Speak affirmations in the present tense, for instance, don't say, "I will be okay," say "I am okay." No matter what the situation speak it in the present tense. When you say, "I will," you are always speaking about the future and the future is always out of reach.

• Affirmations need always infer something positive, don't say, "I am not fat," rather affirm, "My body weight is perfect for optimum health."

• Make your affirmations short phrases that are easily repeated throughout the day.

• Write your affirmations on small post-it pads and stick them everywhere—mirror, fridge, wallet, car console, your computer, eventually just seeing the sticky note will trigger thoughts of your affirmation.

• Some suggested affirmations to create healing thoughts are, "I am lovable, I am enough, and I am worthy."

• Choose one affirmation and stick with it for at least a week. Say it to your self (aloud if possible) as many times as possible. Try saying it a thousand times a day—when you consider we think over 60,000 thoughts a day this is not a lot. In addition, if you repeat it over and over (like a mantra) for about five minutes you will have said it hundreds of times.

• Spend a few minutes repeatedly invoking your affirmation each morning upon waking, again in the middle of the day, and in the evening before going to sleep. Also, say it throughout the day.

• Write any reactions and feelings in your journal.

For the next seven days, I will constantly invoke the following affirmation: (write the same affirmation 52 times)

1. _____

2. _____

3. _____

4. _____

5. _____

6. _____

7. _____

8.   _____

9.   _____

10. _____

11. _____

12. _____

13. _____

14. _____

15. _____

16. _____

17. _____

18. _____

19. _____

20. _____

21. _____

22. _____

23. _____

24. _____

25. _____

26. _____

27. _____

28. _____

29. _____

30. _____

31. _____

32. _____

33. _____

34. _____
35. _____
36. _____
37. _____
38. _____
39. _____
40. _____
41. _____
42. _____
43. _____
44. _____
45. _____
46. _____
47. _____
48. _____
49. _____
50. _____
51. _____
52. _____

Exercise #14: *Your Beliefs About Men*
Free Form Writing

This free form writing exercise deals with your belief system about men. In order to heal we need to become aware of our (sometimes completed outdated) belief system so that we may discard those beliefs that no longer work in our favor. Whether you are male or female, what your deepest beliefs are about men will affect your relationships. What we believe at our deepest level internally will manifest in our lives externally. We have heard for years if we change our belief system we can change our lives. I believe this to be true on many levels.

If you are in a support group, you may do this exercise in your group or as a homework assignment and share your feelings about it with your group. Often if we think we are going to share our response there will be a natural tendency to filter our thoughts. If you are doing group work, make an agreement with the other group members to share your thoughts and feelings about the exercise only—not what you write. This will create a safer environment and allow for more honest venting in the free form writing. Wherever you choose to do this exercise, it is important that you do not change or edit what you wrote when you are done. The only person you have to share it with is you. Remember, the first thoughts that come to your mind are very important and can give you a great deal of insight into yourself.

Write for five to eight minutes every thought that comes to your mind without censoring your words on the following phrase:

What I believe about men is:

_____

_____

_____

_____

_____

_____

_____

_____

- Re-read your response without judgment. Don't be surprised if you responded with some thoughts or beliefs that you were not even aware that you believed in. It is okay, journal about your reaction.

- What belief do you feel no longer serves your highest purpose and you would like to move beyond? Draw a line through those.

- What beliefs would you like to nurture? Circle those.

- Think about what you wrote for a few days and re-visit your response, does your reaction to your response seem to change?

- After a few days re-do the exercise. Write for three to five minutes every thought that comes to your mind.

What I believe about men is:

Is there any difference? If so, what?

_____

_____

_____

_____

_____

Why do you think this is so?

_____

_____

_____

_____

_____

Again, draw a line through the beliefs you would like to eliminate. Circle those beliefs you would like to nurture.

What actions can you take to validate the beliefs you would like to nurture?

_____

_____

_____

_____

_____

_____

_____

Exercise #15: *Your Beliefs About Women*
Free Form Writing

This free form writing exercise deals with your belief system about women. Just as in the previous chapters, it does not matter whether you are male or female what your deepest beliefs are about women will affect your relationships.

If you are in a support group you may do this exercise in your group or as a homework assignment and share your feelings about it with your group. Often if we think we are going to share our response there will be a natural tendency to filter our thoughts. If you are doing group work, make an agreement with the other group members to share your thoughts and feelings about the exercise only—not what you write. This will create a safer environment and allow for more honest venting in the free form writing. Wherever you choose to do this exercise, it is important that you do not change or edit what you wrote when you are done. The only person you have to share it with is you. Remember, the first thoughts that come to our minds are very important and can give us a deal of insight into ourselves.

Write for five to eight minutes every thought that comes to your mind on the following phrase:

What I believe about women is:

_____

_____

_____

_____

_____

_____

_____

_____

_____

_____

_____

_____

_____

_____

_____

_____

_____

_____

_____

_____

_____

- Re-read your response without judgment. Don't be surprised if you responded with some thoughts or beliefs that you were not even aware that you believed in. It is okay, journal about your reaction.

- What belief do you feel no longer serves your highest purpose? Would like to move beyond those outdated beliefs? If so, draw a line through those beliefs you are eliminating.

- What beliefs would you like to nurture? Circle those.

- Think about what you wrote for a few days and re-visit your response, does your reaction to your response seem to change?

- After a few days re-do the exercise. Write for three to five minutes every thought that comes to your mind.

What I believe about women is:

_____

_____

_____

_____

_____

Is there any difference? If so, what?

_____

_____

_____

_____

_____

Why do you think this is so?

_____

_____

_____

_____

_____

Again, draw a line through the beliefs you would like to eliminate. Circle those beliefs you would like to nurture.

What actions can you take to validate the beliefs you would like to nurture?

_____

_____

_____

_____

_____

_____

Exercise #16: *Your Beliefs About Relationships*
Free Form Writing

This free form writing exercise deals with your belief system about relationships. If we are going to have healthier relationships in the future, it is imperative that we began to confront and change our emotional programming and belief system around relationships. What your deepest beliefs are about relationships will affect the quality of all your relationships. What we believe at our deepest level internally will manifest in our lives externally.

If you are in a support group, you may do this exercise in your group or as a homework assignment and share your feelings about it with your group. Often if we think we are going to share our response, there will be a natural tendency to filter our thoughts. If you are doing group work, make an agreement with the other group members to share your thoughts and feelings about the exercise only—not what you write. This will create a safer environment and allow for more honest venting in the free form writing. Wherever you choose to do this exercise, it is important that you do not change or edit what you wrote when you are done. The only person you have to share it with is you. Remember, the first thoughts that come to our minds are very important and can give us a great deal of insight into ourselves.

Write for five to eight minutes every thought that comes to your mind on the following phrase:

What I believe about relationships is:

_____

_____

_____

_____

_____

_____

_____

_____

_____

_____

_____

_____

_____

_____

_____

_____

_____

_____

- Re-read your response without judgment. Don't be surprised if you responded with some thoughts or beliefs that you were not even aware that you believed in. It is okay, journal about your reaction.

- What belief do you feel no longer serves your highest purpose? Would like to move beyond those outdated beliefs? If so, draw a line through those beliefs you are eliminating.

- What beliefs would you like to nurture? Circle those.

- Think about what you wrote for a few days and re-visit your response, does your reaction to your response seem to change?

- After a few days re-do the exercise. Write for three to five minutes every thought that comes to your mind.

What I believe about relationships is:

_____

_____

_____

_____

_____

Is there any difference? If so, what?

_____

_____

_____

_____

_____

Why do you think this is so?

_____

_____

_____

_____

_____

Again, draw a line through the beliefs you would like to eliminate. Circle those beliefs you would like to nurture.

What actions can you take to validate the beliefs you would like to nurture?

_____

_____

_____

_____

_____

_____

_____

Exercise #17: *Relationship Evaluation Mechanism for Your Information (REMY)*

It is important to evaluate our past relationships. An honest evaluation of past relationships can prevent us from continuing to make the same mistakes in the future. The following exercise will help you compare the characteristics of your past relationships so that you may begin to identify your relationship patterns.

The following is a partial list of possible characteristics both positive and negative.

Positive Characteristics

Affectionate	Educated	Independent	Sensitive
Ambitious	Financially Secure	Intelligent	Sexy
Athletic	Flexible	Loves Animals	Sociable
Attentive	Generous	Love Children	Spiritual
Attractive	Gentle Spirit	Mature	Spontaneous
Charming	Giving	Open minded	Stable
Compassionate	Good Parent	Organized	Successful
Conscientious	Great Cook	Outgoing	Supportive
Creative	Honest	Professional	Talented
Dressed Nice	Humorous	Reliable	Wise

Negative Characteristics

Abused Substances	Deceitful	Insecure	Sexual Infidelity
Alcoholic	Depressed	Insensitive	Physically Abusive
Anti-children	Demanding	Intrusive	Sneaky
Anti-Social	Dishonest	Irresponsible	Shopaholic
Arrogant	Domineering	Jealous	Stalker
Angry	Emotionally	Lacks Integrity	Stingy
Cheated	Unavailable	Lazy	Unemotional
Clingy	Fanatic	Married	Unreliable
Compulsive	Fearful	Needy	Verbal Abuse
Control Freak	Flirt	Noncommittal	Victim
Criminal Behavior	Fragile	Obsessive	Violent
Critical	Gambler	Possessive	Vulgar
Deadbeat parent	Incarcerated	Rage-aholic	Workaholic

On the following charts list the names of all significant relationships you have had throughout your entire life. For each significant relationship, list as many characteristics as you can think of. Think about the initial attraction. What was it that attracted you? Why did the relationship end? Include physical characteristics as well (i.e. hair type, height, body type). Summarize the characteristics in as few words as possible. You may use the characteristic list or use your own words. This exercise may take a few days, as you should continue to add to the list as you think of characteristics.

Name:		Name:	
Positive Traits	Negative Traits	Positive Traits	Negative Traits

Name:		Name:	
Positive Traits	Negative Traits	Positive Traits	Negative Traits

After a few days of contemplation and building the inventory, review the entire list and circle those traits both positive and negative that appear in more than one relationship. In the following chart, list the common inventory traits:

Common Traits	
Positive Characteristics	Negative Characteristics

What do you think these common traits say about the type of person that you attract?

_____

_____

_____

_____

Based on this inventory are there things you want to change about the choices you have

made in relationships? If so, what?

_____

_____

_____

_____

_____

_____

In the next chapter, you will have an opportunity to explore further the choices you have
made in relationships.

Exercise #18: *Identify Your Relationship Patterns*

In this exercise, I would like to explore further, why we continue to make the choices we make in relationships. The reality is we choose the people, even if it is subconsciously, that we enter into relationships with based on our emotional programming. Review the recurring characteristics in the previous exercise. It is not a coincidence or bad luck that we continue to attract and/or be attracted to people with very similar characteristics.

All of our relationships are an indicator of what is going on inside of us on a psychological level. It goes back to the most important question to answer if we want to heal. What is it about me that compel me to continue to choose these types of relationships? The answer to this question lies in identifying our relationship patterns.

A number of current relationship theories in use are based on the Adlerian Theory. The Adlerian Theory is a popular psychological theory developed by a well-known psychologist, Dr. Alfred Adler. Dr. Adler theorized that the belief system we have and the choices we make as adults are based on decisions we made as a result of our experiences as young children. Our underlying belief system or emotional programming, influences our thinking, behavior and decision making process. The choices we make in relationships are a result of this emotional programming.

After having made so many bad choices in relationships it was a relief for me to begin to understand that my choices were a result of my emotional programming, which was based on my experiences and not simply the result of having what I referred to as a monster man magnet for a brain. It was a relief to know that I can reprogram my thinking and make healthier choices.

I grew up in an extremely dysfunctional household. My birth was the result of an extramarital affair my mother had with my biological father. My mother then separated from her husband and became the single parent of five, then six, then seven, then eight, then nine children. My mother worked hard to provide for us but she was never emotionally or physically affectionate. My biological father was irresponsible and never provided financial support. He was in and out of my life the first eight years and then I did not see him anymore until I was eighteen. He was an alcoholic and a womanizer, who fathered children from at least seven different women. However, on the positive side my father was very handsome, always dressed nice, very charming, a good conversationalist and always the life of the party. I was also sexually abused during the years of my father's absence and I was afraid to tell my mother.

I began to make some decisions based on my experience during my childhood. I decided men have the power, they are unavailable, and they do not have to be responsible. I decided women cannot be trusted, that women are cold and distant, that women are the weaker sex, and that women are less valuable than men. My belief system about life in general developed into, life is unfair, life is hard work, and expect constant disappointment. My core belief system about myself, basically, amounted to I was unworthy and unlovable. When I looked at the choices I made in my relationship inventory, it became obvious to me that I was acting out my emotional programming by validating my belief system. I subconsciously sought out relationships that would validate exactly what I believed based on my emotional programming. Once I understood why I made such choices, I was free to make different choices.

In the following exercise you will began to examine your emotional programming which are the decisions that you have made based on your experiences that have created your core beliefs. Use this chart to examine your emotional programming. For example, if I were to chart the above-mentioned experience it would look similar to the following.

Experience	Decisions	Core Beliefs	Relationship Choices
Father womanizer very charming yet unavailable. Mother hard worker, but emotionally distant	Men are unavailable; Women are weaker and cannot be trusted, Life is hard and unfair.	I am not worthy I am not lovable	Emotionally distant or unavailable men. All very attractive, nice dressers, charming, and irresponsible.

1. Think about your painful childhood experiences (i.e. parents divorced, death in family, alcohol or substance abuse in family, chaotic family environment, sexual, physical, emotional, or verbal abuse, poverty, etc.). List those in column #1.

2. What decisions did you make about others or life based on the experience? List those in column #2.

3. What core belief did you develop about yourself based on your experiences and the decisions you made? List those in column #3.

4. Review your relationship inventory. What relationship choices did you make based on your emotional programming? List those in column #4.

5. Allow yourself a few days to do this exercise so that you may give yourself the opportunity to process. Use your journal and support system to share the feelings that may surface as you begin to examine painful childhood experiences.

Experience	Decisions	Core Beliefs	Relationship Choices

Experience	Decisions	Core Beliefs	Relationship Choices

The preceding exercise has given you the opportunity to identify the emotional programming that created our relationship choices. In the following exercise you will began the process of reprogramming. To do this we will use the power of the affirming word. My core belief about myself was I am unworthy. The affirmation that I used to reprogram my thinking was, "I am worthy." This affirming word became action in my life as I began to accomplish things that I previously thought myself unworthy of in the past. I demonstrated my new belief system by doing major things for myself such as registering for college and applying for a promotion at my job. I also demonstrated my new belief system in smaller ways such as exercising, eating healthy, or buying myself something nice.

1. In column #1 list the core beliefs you developed about yourself based on your emotional programming.
2. What affirmations could you use to overcome the negative belief? In most cases you could simply say the opposite in an affirming way (reverse, "I am not lovable" to "I am lovable"). Although you may find it difficult to believe your affirming words, go through the process and it will get easier to believe overtime. Write your affirming words in column #2.
3. What action can you take to demonstrate you belief in your affirming words? This is the most important step in the reprogramming because it provides validation of your new belief. List your actions in column #3.
4. Continue to repeat your affirming words to yourself and everyday look for ways to validate your new belief.

Old Belief	New Belief	New Belief Demonstrated by

Exercise # 19: *52 Reasons to be Grateful*

I was not only filled with sadness after my divorce I was filled with a litany of complaints. I had the full responsibility for managing the household. I had to buy the groceries, cook the meals, and wash the dishes. Take out the trash, pump the gas, and wash the car. I felt overwhelmed with resentment each time I did a chore that my ex-husband had done in the past.

One day as I was cutting the grass with tears of anger and frustration rolling down my face I had an epiphany. As I was whining and complaining about having to cut the grass, it dawned on me that I had grass to cut. I had a yard, which meant I had a house! I wondered how many people would love to have this problem right now. Moreover, I found gratitude! Here I was mumbling and grumbling about doing a chore that in all reality was a blessing to be able to do. My entire attitude shifted. I began to be grateful to have the bills because they meant I had some <u>things</u> such as hot water, and air conditioning and luxury items that I take for granted like a cell phone or cable TV. I began to see the blessings in all things, and situations that seemed burdensome became an opportunity to give thanks.

No matter what is going on in our lives there is always something to be grateful for. When relationships hurt, it may be difficult to acknowledge the good things in our lives. However, it is now more important than ever to acknowledge the good. It is difficult if not impossible to entertain a pity party or nurse resentment when we are being grateful.

Self-pity like depression creates a negative energy that attaches itself to your surroundings. If you are in self-pity or feeling a little blue it is important to <u>move.</u> Get out the bed! Get off the couch! Take a shower! Walk outside! Open the window! <u>MOVE.</u> Force yourself to think about the good (i.e. you have eyes to read this; you had money to purchase the book, or someone cared enough about you to give you a copy).

On the following page, create your gratitude list of 52 reasons to be grateful. Think about your life, no matter how bad things are right now there are still reasons to be grateful. Did you have a good meal? Do you have hot water? Are you able to walk up a flight of stairs? Did you have clean towels or fresh sheets? You have eyes to read and you have the willingness to heal.

Write your list. The first few things may come easily off the top of your head, and then you will have to THINK about the GOOD in your life, changing your focus (and your energy) from negative to positive. If you are unable to think of 52 things today, use the next few days and continue to add to your gratitude list.

As you continue to move through the healing process, make it a habit to do a small gratitude list everyday by writing at least five reasons you are grateful in your journal.

1. _____
2. _____
3. _____
4. _____
5. _____
6. _____
7. _____
8. _____
9. _____
10. _____
11. _____
12. _____
13. _____
14. _____
15. _____
16. _____
17. _____
18. _____
19. _____
20. _____
21. _____
22. _____
23. _____
24. _____
25. _____
26. _____

27. _____
28. _____
29. _____
30. _____
31. _____
32. _____
33. _____
34. _____
35. _____
36. _____
37. _____
38. _____
39. _____
40. _____
41. _____
42. _____
43. _____
44. _____
45. _____
46. _____
47. _____
48. _____
49. _____
50. _____
51. _____
52. _____

Exercise #20: *Dealing With The Disappointment*

When we feel disappointment, it is an indicator of not getting our expectations met. When we have expectations that are not met, we feel disappointment. Sometimes our expectations are reasonable and we should expect to have our needs met. At other times, our expectations are unreasonable and we set ourselves up for disappointment. Then there are those times when the expectations are reasonable, but we place the expectation on someone who is constitutionally incapable of meeting our needs. For instance, we have a right to honesty and to be treated with respect. But we may place this expectation on someone who has no history of being honest or respectful. We are then disappointed in that person when they do not meet our expectations.

Basically, people are who they are and they behave according to their own personal standards. The problem is we often expect people to behave according to our standards and when they don't we take it personally and we feel disappointment. I was very disappointed when my ex-husband behaved selfishly and became self-involved during our marriage; however I began to realize he was merely being who he was. He had no history of being responsible, nor did he have any experience considering the feelings and circumstances of others, yet I expected him to be able to do so simply because we were married.

The parable of the man and the snake is a perfect example of how we place expectations on people who are unable to meet them. In this parable, the man is walking down a road when he happens upon a snake that is lying injured in the road. The snake begs the man to help him by moving him out of the road. He was afraid that the snake would bite, so, the man was reluctant about picking it up. The snake convinced the man that he would not harm him and he would be so grateful if he would help. The man picked up the snake and put him in his pocket. He carried him around and nursed him back to health. As he was about to release the snake onto his path, the snake turned around and bit the man. The man was shocked, hurt, and confused. He asked the snake, "How could you bite me after I trusted you?" The snake merely replied, "Because I am a snake."

In what ways do you feel disappointed?

Have you ever felt disappointed about something similar before?

Describe

_____

_____

_____

_____

We cannot feel disappointment unless there were some expectations. State clearly and precisely what your expectations were.

_____

_____

_____

_____

_____

Did you state clearly and precisely your expectation?

If the answer is no, why not?

_____

_____

_____

_____

_____

Do you believe people can meet your needs even if you do not state clearly what they are?

_____

_____

_____

_____

If you did state your expectations very clearly, think about your REMY[1], could that person realistically meet your expectations?

_____

_____

_____

_____

_____

What can you learn from this situation?

_____

_____

_____

_____

What are you willing to do differently in the future to have your needs met?

_____

_____

_____

_____

_____

[1]Relationship Evaluation Mechanism for Your Information, or the person you were/are in a relationship with.

Exercise #21: *Its Okay If You're Angry*

As you move through the stages of grief when relationships hurt, don't be surprised to find yourself feeling tremendous anger. Most often anger is a secondary feeling, meaning it is felt in response to a primary feeling. The primary feeling is usually hurt, disappointment, rejection or some emotion of that nature. However, those emotions can leave us feeling extremely vulnerable. Anger on the other hand is a more powerful emotion. Some may feel more in control when angry, and others may feel out of control when angry. Anger is simply indignation at a perceived wrong and there are times when we have a right to be angry. Anger is a normal and natural emotion when relationships hurt.

In the cases where we are afraid of our anger, we are more likely to stuff our anger. We may become numb and not feel anger or any other emotion we can identify. Dealing with the anger is a good way to start making room for the other emotions to surface as we move towards healing. Since depression is often described as anger turned inwards, it is important to deal with the anger, otherwise, we may begin to feel depressed or self-pity.

Some suggestions for dealing with your anger include the following:

- Write an angry letter to your REMY[1], (this maybe a, "dead" letter, that you may not actually give to your REMY; however, write it as if you are). The healing is in the purging. Be very clear in the letter what you are angry about and why. Also, state what your expectations were. When you are done, you may burn, shred, or bury the letter. You may also store it in your journal as a reminder to yourself when selective memory kicks in and you can only remember the wonderful times you have had with your REMY.

- Draw or paint a picture to express your anger.

- Write a poem. A very expressive poem.

- Carve or build something out of wood

- Sponge-paint a room/wall in your house. Really slap that paint on!

- Shout with as much force as possible "I am angry," repeat at least seven times (make sure you are in a safe place, such as a parked car with windows rolled up) or alone at home.

- Have a temper tantrum. Lie on the floor, wail your arms, kick your legs and scream, "I am angry!"

- Kick, pound, or hit a beanbag—forcefully say, "I am angry."

---

[1] <u>R</u>elationship <u>E</u>valuation <u>M</u>echanism for <u>Y</u>our Information, or the person you were/are in a relationship with.

- Beat a pillow or bed with a plastic bat.

- Physical exercise such as jogging to maximum exertion level.

- Pound nails into a wood surface

- Tape a picture of your REMY under your shoes and walk around, squash your REMY's face in the ground all day (trust me this is healthier than actually taking your anger out on your REMY.

- Post your REMY in the REMY database at whenrelationshipshurt.com. Being able to vent to others about your REMY is often therapeutic.

Complete the following exercises:

The situation I am angry about is (what specifically are you angry at?)

_____

_____

_____

_____

I feel angry at this situation because (why does this situation make you angry?)

_____

_____

_____

_____

Because of this situation, I have (what ways have you acted out because of your anger?)

_____

_____

_____

_____

Because of this situation I believe (what do you believe about relationships, life, yourself, etc.?)

_____

_____

_____

_____

This belief helps or hurts me in the following ways

_____

_____

_____

_____

The best thing I can do for myself when I am angry is (how will you express your anger?)

_____

_____

_____

_____

Exercise #22: *Moving Through the Blame*

I had plenty of fuel. My ex-husband had an affair during our marriage. He told countless lies and more lies to cover lies. He emotionally abandoned me after I received a cancer diagnosis and went through a year of doctor appointments, surgeries, and hospitalizations. He got lost in his gambling addiction, gambled our entire savings, maxed out the credit cards, and took out loans that he did not repay. Following an arrest, his termination from a very lucrative job furthered my humiliation. Oh yes I had plenty to blame him for.

However, it occurred to me that if I only focused on his wrongs, I would never get better. My blaming him was counter-productive in my healing process. I knew who my ex-husband was when I married him; after all I was marrying him for the second time. I chose to marry him not based on who he was but rather based on his potential. I was responding to my hidden fears and he was safe because he was familiar. I made some bad choices, and as long as I was blaming him, I could not take responsibility for my piece.

While blaming the other person for your hurt and disappointment may bring some amount of satisfaction, it is counter-productive to the healing process. The reason blaming does not help you in your healing is because as long as it is his or her fault and he or she is the one wrong then it is only the other person that need to change. Since you are powerless over creating the change in the other person, you will never get the result you want. However, if you began to take some responsibility for the situation you have the power to change you. Even if your only responsibility is, you made a bad choice, by acknowledging this; you have the power to make different choices. Taking responsibility empowers us to create changes to help us heal when relationships hurt.

1. What are you blaming your REMY[1] for?

_____

_____

_____

2. What have you done to repay your REMY for what you feel he/she has done?

_____

_____

_____

[1]Relationship Evaluation Mechanism for Your Information, or the person you were/are in a relationship with.

3. What ways have you hurt yourself as a result of what your REMY did?

_____

_____

_____

4. For what situations are you willing to take responsibility?

_____

_____

_____

5. What are you willing to do to make amends with your REMY?

_____

_____

_____

6. What are you willing to do to make amends with yourself?

_____

_____

_____

Exercise #23: *Allow Yourself to Feel Sad*

When relationships hurt, we need to give ourselves permission to grieve. Grief happens in stages and may include denial, sadness, anger, and acceptance. Of course, there may be other variations of grief such as guilt, disappointment, or blame. There is no set order or length for each stage. My suggestion is to stay in touch with your emotions through journaling and sharing your feelings with trusted others. Allow yourself to process through each emotion as they surface.

Part of dealing with the grief is feeling the sadness. If you are not in a supportive environment you may feel you should be over the sadness in a few weeks, and as a result of feeling unsupported you may spend a lot of time stuffing or avoiding the sadness. I have had people say to me, "I have cried about it for an hour or I cried all night, I don't understand why I still feel so sad." We are so accustomed to instant gratification and in the last few decades, have become such an instantaneous society in everything from instant meals to instant mail. We expect all of life including our emotions to operate instantly. We've gotten to the point where we are almost embarrassed to let people know that we are still grieving the ending of a relationship even after just a few weeks.

However, when relationships hurt it may take months or even years to move through the sadness. I spent two years after my divorce feeling a lot of sadness. Despite the pain of the relationship, I missed him. I longed for his presence. I felt sad when I went to bed and sad when I woke up. I embraced my sadness because I knew in a place of deep knowing that this too shall pass. I did not resist the sadness and I found that I was able to function quite successfully in my life by acknowledging the sadness. I recognized that I had many reasons to feel sadness and I needed to honor my feelings.

The dissolution of my marriage brought up every hurt and disappointment I had felt my entire life. This will often happen when we are grieving because I have found that sadness is an emotion that defies time and circumstance, and it will connect to all unresolved grief. When relationships hurt, we may find ourselves feeling sadness about things that happened decades before. I found myself grieving things like my last doll baby that my little brother destroyed or my friend that died when I was in middle school. I grieved the loss of every relationship I'd ever had. I grieved things I never had like a daddy when I was a little girl to show me what love from a man was suppose to feel like. I felt sadness because as soon as I got to know my daddy and feel his love he died. I missed him and I missed everyone close to me that was deceased or who had moved away.

Some suggestions for dealing with the sadness are:

- Journal, journal, journal!

- Give yourself permission to be sad

- Write a 'dead' letter (a letter you do <u>not</u> mail, but write for healing purpose) to your REMY[1] describing your sadness. Go into details of your grief.

- CRY!!! CRY!!! CRY!!! And CRY some more!!! It's okay. The tears are healing!!

- Complete the when relationships hurt collage (exercise #12)

- Watch a DVD of your favorite comedian (or have a friend recommend one) laugh out loud at the funny parts

- Throw yourself a pity party

  o Invite a few supportive and understanding friends to your party that are totally willing to indulge you.

  o Spend one hour sitting on the pity pot (place a stool or ottoman in the center of the group), bewail all of your sorrows and woes, whine as much as you like during this time. If you are in a support group—the entire group can be dedicated to a group pity party.

  o At the end of the allotted time dry your eyes (if any tears are left), and announce your commitment to get on with the business of living.

  o When you get up off the pot, don't forget to flush.

I am sad because (don't forget to list any unresolved sadness or grief from the past that maybe showing up during this time):

_____

_____

_____

_____

_____

_____

[1]<u>R</u>elationship <u>E</u>valuation <u>M</u>echanism for <u>Y</u>our Information, or the person you were/are in a relationship with.

_____

_____

_____

_____

The way I have dealt with my sadness in the past is by:

_____

_____

_____

_____

_____

_____

_____

_____

_____

The best way I can deal with my sadness now is:

_____

_____

_____

_____

_____

_____

_____

Exercise #24: *Confronting Your Fear(s)*

Fear is the most powerful human emotion there is and it is the underlying principle for all negative behaviors. There are only two primary principles that govern everything that we think, feel, or do. Those two primary principles are fear and love. These two principles govern everything that happens on this planet. Wars are fought because of fear. Refugee camps are set up because of love. People are starving on this planet because of fear and the hungry are fed because of love. We stay in and return to unhealthy relationships because of fear. We let go because of love.

Fear will often disguise itself as love with thoughts such as "you can't leave me, I need you, I have to have you." These are not love-based thoughts but rather fear-based thoughts that manifest through jealousy, possessiveness, control, and obsession. Fear produces all negative thoughts and behaviors such as denial, resentments, manipulation, dishonesty, judgments, gluttony, and envy. All negative thoughts and behaviors are simply, "defense mechanisms," we use to protect ourselves from our perceived fears. Of all emotions fear is the most controlling, and it keeps us trapped in the past and attached to the pain. On the other hand, love produces thoughts and behaviors such as honesty, acceptance, trust, tolerance, compassion, willingness, and courage. While you may have genuine love for someone it could be tainted with fear-based emotions.

The best way to deal with fear is:

#1 Acknowledge It
Remember fear has many manifestations. When we are not being honest or trying to control a situation what is really going on is fear. Admit that. When you recognize any negative thoughts or behaviors ask yourself, "What am I afraid of?" Bringing the fear to your conscious mind positions you to deal with the fear.

#2 Understand It
Where does this fear come from? Most fears are based on past experiences. They may have had some validity at some point in our lives but we keep re-creating those negative situations through our fears. My father was not there for me as a child. Consequently, I developed a belief system that said I was not worthy of love and my core fear was rejection and/or abandonment. I began to develop behaviors to defend myself against these fears such as manipulation and self-compromising behaviors.

#3 Deal with it
Write about the emotions, thoughts or behaviors that you are aware of as a result of you fear. Write about where you feel your fears are coming from. Share these with someone in your support system. Develop a plan to move through the fear.

#4 Confront it

Just do it. Do that thing that you are afraid of, look fear in the eye and say, "I recognize you as fear and I am moving through my fear." Remember that courage is not lack of fear but the ability to move even when we feel afraid.

Some common fears we experience when relationships hurt are:

- We are afraid of being rejected

- We are afraid these feelings will last forever

- We are afraid we will never love again

- We are afraid we will never be happy again

- We are afraid of conflict

What are your fears? List all you can think of.

I am afraid of _____

I am afraid of _____

I am afraid of _____

I am afraid of _____

I am afraid of _____

Where does the fear come from? Often your fears are based on your beliefs about you or about life. It is important to understand where the fear is coming from.

This fear comes from my belief that _____

This fear comes from my belief that _____

This fear comes from my belief that _____

This fear comes from my belief that _____

This fear comes from my belief that _____

How do you respond when you are afraid? For instance, do you become judgmental, do you attempt to control, do you isolate, do you compromise, etc.

What I do when I am afraid is: _____

What I do when I am afraid is: _____

What I do when I am afraid is: _____

What I do when I am afraid is: _____

What I do when I am afraid is: _____

How can you confront your fear(s)? Doing the opposite of what you would normally do when you are afraid is often a good way to confront your fears. (i.e. attend social functions, spend the weekend alone, etc.)

I will confront my fear by: _____

I will confront my fear by: _____

I will confront my fear by: _____

I will confront my fear by: _____

I will confront my fear by: _____

Affirmations are a powerful tool to utilize when confronting fear. Some example affirmations are:

- I am safe

- It is safe to be who I am

- I am worthy

- All is well in my world

- Life lovingly supports me

- I am protected by divine presence

- I make right choices

- I am a loving child of God

- I am great to be around

Exercise #25: *Forgive your REMY!*

If you have done the exercises on disappointment, anger, blame, sadness and fear you are now ready to move on to forgiveness. If you have not done the above exercises, I strongly suggest that you do so before doing this one.

Forgiveness does not mean you endorse the wrong doings of others. Forgiveness does mean you let go of the judgment. As long as you are still angry and resentful towards someone, you cannot let go. Holding onto anger and resentment actually does you more harm than the person with whom you are angry. Lack of forgiveness keeps you attached emotionally to that person, and they own a piece of you. Until you let go you cannot create room for something new.

Forgiveness does not mean you continue to accept unacceptable behaviors, but rather you establish clear boundaries and move on. Forgiveness does not invalidate your feelings, but confirms your right to be free of other people issues.

Forgiveness Exercises

Purchase a large helium filled balloon. On separate pieces of paper write the words "ANGER," "SADNESS," "DISAPPOINTMENT," "FEAR," and "BLAME," tape each word securely to the balloon, on another sheet of paper write:

Dear _____,
I now forgive you for the disappointment, anger, and sadness (or any other feelings) you have caused me. I release the blame and I move through the fear. I forgive you and I set you free and in doing so I release me and set me free.

Tape a note to balloon and release it in an open area (avoid trees, power lines, etc). Watch the balloon as it rises and fades from view. Repeating, "I release and let go." Pay attention to the feelings that surface during this exercise. Share those feelings with someone in your support group or write about them in your journal.

Repeat the above phrase at least twice a day for the next seven days. Be sure to continue journaling any feelings/reactions to exercise.

Is there something specific you are having a hard time letting go? List those things:

_____   _____

_____   _____

_____   _____

[1]Relationship Evaluation Mechanism for Your Information, or the person you were/are in a relationship with.

I am holding on to this because:

_____

_____

_____

_____

I have believed if I let go of this it will mean:

_____

_____

_____

_____

I now realize if I let go it will help me in the following ways:

_____

_____

_____

_____

I now choose to let go of the following emotions or situations:

_____

_____

_____

_____

You might want to repeat the balloon exercise on the seventh day and release any residual emotions.

Do this exercise as often as necessary as you move through the resentments and anger when relationships hurt.

Exercise #26: *Forgive Yourself*

Just as importantly as forgiving our REMY, we need also to forgive ourselves. Frequently when relationships hurt, we are angry with ourselves for making poor choices or for being a "fool in love." We berate ourselves over and over for making mistakes. We are often our harshest critics and our toughest judge. We often think, "if only…. I should have…" and the list goes on and on.

Yes, we may have made some mistakes and some poor choices. But how long must we condemn ourselves? The bottom line is that whatever happened has already happened and it cannot be undone now. The past is the past and wallowing in regret will only keep us fixed in the pain. We are often more forgiving of others than we are of ourselves. Our healing process requires that we move from a place of self-condemnation to a place of compassion and forgiveness towards ourselves.

Sometimes we may not be aware of our lack of self-forgiveness as it may show up in subtle ways such as:

- How we treat our bodies, the foods we eat, our grooming and hygiene, the clothes we wear;

- Clutter and disorganization in our living and work environment;

- Self sabotaging behaviors such as oversleeping on the day of the big presentation;

- Using a lot of sarcasm and cynicism;

- We push ourselves to the limits, demanding total perfection from ourselves.

- We become fanatics with religion, exercise, or etc.

- We accept unacceptable behaviors from others. We may be passive or passive-aggressive and do not speak up for ourselves.

- We abuse alcohol and/or drugs, or have other addictive behaviors such as shopping, gambling, or overeating.

Any of the above behaviors indicate a need for self-forgiveness. For what situations do you need to forgive yourself? Please do not limit yourself to situations around your REMY[1]

---

[1] <u>R</u>elationship <u>E</u>valuation <u>M</u>echanism for <u>Y</u>our Information, or the person you were/are in a relationship with.

_____

_____

_____

_____

_____

_____

_____

_____

Write the following letter to yourself.

Dear _____ _____,

I now forgive myself for any decisions or choices I may have made. I now understand that no relationships are failures if we learn from them. I am learning and growing everyday as a result of this experience. For that, I am grateful. I release judgment and self-condemnation so that I may continue to move forward towards my future without being chained to my past.

Love, _____ _____

Tape this letter to a helium-filled balloon. Tape the words shame, guilt, and disappointment to the balloon. Write down any other situation you need to forgive yourself for and tape it to the balloon. Release the balloon in an open area (avoid trees, power lines, etc). Watch the balloon as it rises and fades from view. Repeating, "I release and let go." Pay attention to the feelings that surface during this exercise. Share those feelings with someone in your support group or write about them in your journal.

Repeat the above phrase at least twice a day for the next seven days. Be sure to continue journaling any feelings/reactions to exercise.

Put the following affirmations on post-it-notes and post in visible locations for the next seven days:

- I forgive myself for the choices I have made

- No relationships are failures if we learn from them

Is there something specific you are having a hard time letting go of? List those things:

_____   _____
_____   _____
_____   _____

I am holding on to this because:

_____

_____

_____

I have believed if I let go of this it will mean:

_____

_____

_____

I now realize if I let go it will help me in the following ways:

_____

_____

_____

I now choose to let go of the following emotions or situations:

_____

_____

_____

You might want to repeat the balloon exercise on the 7th day and release any residual emotions.
Do this exercise as often as necessary as you work on forgiving yourself.

Exercise #27: *Pampering*

Most adults do not spend enough time in self-loving, self-nurturing, pampering acts. There are so many demands placed on our time and energy. Some days it seems that we barely have time to eat and it seems impossible to set aside time to pamper ourselves. But just as important as food and water is to the body so is pampering to the mind and spirit.

When we engage in activities of self-pampering, it sends deep messages of self-love to our subconscious mind. It will literally begin to re-program our subconscious mind with life-affirming thoughts such as:

- I am worthy

- I am loved

- I am cared for

- I deserve good things

The following are some examples of pampering acts we can do to help nurture our body, mind, and spirit:

- If you are in a support group dedicate at least one group to pampering each other with neck, hand, or foot massages, and other pampering activities.

- Light scented candles or burn aromatherapy oils. Splurge on something other than the discount store brand, the difference will be well worth it.

- Play soft jazz music or nature sounds CDs.

- Take hot baths. Use your favorite aromatherapy oils. Spend at least twenty minutes soaking away stress, doubt, and fear.

- Give yourself a pedicure or even better have it done by a professional. Make sure they have a heated massage chair to increase your pampering experience.

- Prepare a candlelight dinner—for yourself or invite a friend from your support group and share the pampering.

- Make yourself a cup of hot herbal tea or my favorite is a chai tea latte.

- Get a facial. This is good for both men and women. Guys if you always shave let someone else do it.

- Buy yourself a new outfit. Dress up in the middle of the week without a reason and embrace the compliments you receive.

- Buy yourself new undergarments. Make them really nice and sexy. Don't wait for a special occasion to wear them, but wear them for you on an ordinary day.

- Use the good china. What are you saving it for?

- Wear your best cologne/perfume. Again, What are you saving it for?

- Purchase a set of Egyptian cotton sheets.

- Buy yourself new bath towels.

- Buy yourself flowers.

- Go card shopping for you and mail yourself a greeting card.

- Make yourself a special dessert.

- Get a full body massage.

- Plan a date with yourself doing exactly what you like to do.

- Start a pampering fund. Save a few dollars each week towards a pampering goal.

Spend the next seven days performing at least one pampering act for yourself each day. What are you willing to do over the next seven days to pamper yourself? Be very specific, set the day and time if appropriate.

Day #1

_____

_____

_____

Day #2

_____

_____

_____

Day #3

_____

_____

_____

Day #4

_____

_____

_____

Day #5

_____

_____

_____

Day #6

_____

_____

_____

Day #7

_____

_____

_____

After seven days, complete the following phrase:
I understand pampering to be important to my self-worth because

_____

_____

_____

Exercise #28: *52 Ways to Reduce Stress*

When our emotions are fragile, such as during the times we are dealing with the pain from a relationship, our ability to deal with the day-to-day stress of life decreases. It would be nice if the world would just stop moving while we go through our process, but that is not going to happen. Unfortunately, there are still meals to prepare, presentations to present, laundry to be done, homework to be checked, buses to catch, and dishes to wash. There are rainy days, bad drivers, inept cashiers, long lines, and flat tires. Life continues to show up and doesn't need our permission to do so.

What is going to be important is developing healthy ways to help us manage the day-to-day stresses in our lives. The primary tool for stress management is to recognize the situations in our lives that we have no control over and are unable to change such as long lines and traffic jams. Rather than exerting useless energy towards something we are powerless to change, it is more reasonable to focus our energy on changing our response to the situation. For instance, if you are caught in a traffic jam, there isn't an amount of yelling, screaming, or horn honking that will change the flow of traffic. It will only succeed in sending your stress level through the car roof. On the other hand, you do have some control over and can change your perception of the situation and how you deal with it. Rather than getting angry, you can choose to be grateful that you are safe and not involved in the accident or whatever is causing the traffic jam. You can take this time to sort out your thoughts, to talk with God, repeat your affirmations, or to listen to positive and uplifting music. Don't forget to share your good mood by smiling at your fellow travelers.

The following is a list of 52 Proven Ways to Reduce Stress (some taken from the American Heart Association—Stress Management). You will need a highlighter and as you read slowly through the list, highlight those suggestions that you can apply to your life to help reduce stress.

52 Ways to Reduce Stress
(Some taken from The American Heart Association)

1. Get up fifteen minutes earlier in the morning, and your entire morning will be less stressful.

2. Learn the art of saying, "no." Saying no to extra projects, social activities, and invitations takes courage, discipline, and self-respect. Remember, 'no' is a complete sentence.

3. Relax your standards. The world will not end if the grass is not mowed this weekend, or the dishes not washed tonight.

4. Everyday, do something you really enjoy.

5. Get enough sleep. Set an alarm clock to remind you to go to bed.

6. Prepare for the morning the evening before. Make your lunch; iron your clothes, etc.

7. Go to sleep and wake up at the same time everyday. This creates structure.

8. Learn to live one day at a time. Today is the only day we really have—yesterday is history and tomorrow is a mystery! Fretting about the past or worrying about the future only creates unnecessary stress.

9. Turn off the television and enjoy the quiet. Listen to soothing, "stress free" music.

10. Plan ahead. Don't let the gas tank get below one-quarter full; don't wait until you are down to your last bus token or postage stamp to buy more, etc.

11. Temporarily disconnect. Unplug the phone or get an answering machine.

12. Get up and stretch periodically if you sit for extended periods.

13. Wear earplugs. Noisy environment, can't find a quiet space? Earplugs work.

14. Do something nice for someone else. Taking the focus off of you is a great stress reducer.

15. Procrastination is stressful. Whatever you want to do tomorrow, do today; whatever you want to do today, do it now.

16. Don't rely on your memory; buy a pocket calendar. (Old proverb: A short pencil is better than a long memory.)

17. Go for a walk on the beach, in a park, or around your block—just walk it off.

18. Eliminate (or restrict) the amount of caffeine in your diet

19. Drive at or under the speed limit. Give yourself an extra fifteen minutes to reach appointments. Plan to arrive at airports an hour and half before domestic departures.

20. Close you eyes for a few moments (obviously at a safe opportunity), breath deeply through your nose to the count of eight. Then with lips puckered, exhale very slowly through your mouth to the count of sixteen, or for as long as you can. Concentrate on the long sighing sound and feel the tension dissolve. Repeat this exercise a few times.

21. Always have a backup plan, "just incase..." "(If for some reason one of us is delayed, here's what we'll do...)"

22. Writing your thoughts and feelings down (in a journal, or on a paper to be thrown away) can help you clarify things and can give you a renewed perspective.

23. Count your blessings. For every one thing that goes wrong there is probably fifty blessings. Count them.

24. Don't be afraid to ask questions. Repeat directions and phone numbers.

25. Turn 'needs' into preferences. Our basic physical need translates into food, water, and keeping warm. Everything else is a preference. Don't get attached to preferences.

26. Simplify your life. Remember KISS: Keep It Simple Sweetie.

27. Make friends with non-worriers. Nothing can get you into the habit of worrying faster than associating with chronic worrywarts.

28. Take a hot bath or shower (or cool one in summer) to relieve tension.

29. Create order out of chaos. Organize your home and workspace so that you know where things are. Put things where they belong and you won't have to go through the stress of looking for them.

30. Check your breathing throughout the day, and before, during and afterwards high stress situations. If you find your stomach muscles knotted and your breathing shallow, relax all your muscles and take several deep, slow breaths.

31. Make duplicates of all keys. Keep them in a safe accessible place; give the duplicates to trusted others.

32. Exercise regularly. The toxins that build up in our body as a result of stress are released when we exercise.

33. Talk it out. Discussing your problems with a trusted friend can help clear your mind of confusion so you can concentrate on problem solving. A problem shared is a problem lessened.

34. Do something that will improve your appearance. Do your nails, get a haircut, play with make-up or clip those nose hairs. Looking better will help you feel better.

35. Schedule a realistic day. Avoid the tendency to schedule back-to-back appointments; allow time between appointments for a breathing spell.

36. Become more flexible. Some things are worth not doing perfectly and some issues are well to compromise upon.

37. Set small manageable goals. Save up the pennies and the dollars will take care of themselves.

38. Do one thing at a time. When you are with someone, be with that person and no one or nothing else. When you are busy with a project, concentrate on doing that project and forget about everything else you have to do.

39. Do unpleasant tasks early in the day and get them over with, then the rest of your day will be free from anxiety.

40. Learn to delegate responsibilities to capable others.

41. Don't forget to take a lunch break. Try to get away from your desk or work area in body and mind, even if it's just for fifteen or twenty minutes.

42. Forget counting to ten. Count to 1,000 before doing or saying something that could make matters worse.

43. Have a forgiving view of events and people. Accept the fact that we live in an imperfect world.

44. Have an optimistic view of life. Believe that most people are doing the best they can.

45. Don't sweat the small stuff.

46. Practice preventive maintenance. Your car or appliances are less likely to break down, "at the worst possible moment."

47. Eliminate destructive self-talk: "I'm too old…, I'm too fat…" etc.

48. Be prepared to wait. A paperback can make a wait in the doctor's office almost pleasant.

49. For a change of pace, do something else for a while when the stress of getting the job done gets in the way.

50. Don't put up with something that doesn't work right. If your alarm clock, windshield wipers—or whatever—are a constant aggravation, get them fixed or get new ones.

51. Keep the big picture in mind. Sometimes, we need to step back to see the forest when the trees in front of us block our view.

52. Add an ounce of love to everything you do. After all, you are doing it anyways.

Now that you have read the 52 Proven Ways to Reduce Stress, it's time to take the suggestions and personalize them to your life. Think about the suggestions you highlighted. How can you personally apply them to your life over the next seven days to reduce stress? Write the suggestions as personalized statements. (See my examples below). Make sure to follow the suggestions in the next seven days to help reduce stress. Chose at least twelve suggestions.

Suggestion #	**Personal Stress Reducer**
Examples:	
1	I will get up at 5:45 Rather than 6:00 a.m.
28	I will clean out the storage drawers in my kitchen
41	I will allow my son to choose his own clothes for the week

Exercise #29: *Take Time to Play*

Life never seems more serious than when we are dealing with emotional pain. Yet it is during this time that having fun is most important to bring balance to our emotions. When is the last time you played? Not basketball or tennis, but really played. When was the last time you sat down on the floor or the ground and played with the abandonment of a child? Well there is an inner child in all of us that would love an opportunity to express him/herself through play. Life is serious enough. There is always some responsibility that we have to take care of. Don't worry it will still be there when you are done playing.

As adults, we can become very rigid and lose the spontaneity of our childhood. Think about your childhood. What were some of your favorite childhood toys/games?

What type of things did you do for fun?

_____

_____

_____

What are the reasons you tell yourself that you no longer do those things?

_____

_____

_____

_____

How does it feel when you think about doing these fun things now as an adult? What emotions surface?

_____

_____

_____

_____

What other fun activities can you do?

_____

_____

_____

_____

Go to a discount store or even better go to a toy store and purchase yourself a few toys. Not the grownup computerized toys, but real old-fashioned toys such as Jack Stones, Coloring Books and Crayons, Barbie Dolls with extra outfits, water guns, Lego sets or other building blocks. The toys I will purchase/have purchased for myself are:

_____

_____

_____

_____

What other fun activities can you do?

_____

_____

_____

_____

Set aside at least an hour of uninterrupted time. Take off the stuffy shirt and tie, the pantyhose and high heels. Put on some comfortable old clothes or pajamas and a pair of cotton socks. Get down on the floor and play without an agenda, without competing, play simply for the sake of playing. If you have children, invite them to play with you.

How does it feel to play again?

_____

_____

_____

_____

Exercise #30: *Self-Discovery*

When relationships hurt, we may find ourselves feeling wounded and alone. It is important that we began to develop relationships that nurture us and help us to heal. One of the most important relationships that need to be nurtured is the one with your self.

How well do you know yourself? How much thought or energy do you give to getting to know your self? We often spend more time getting to know a perfect stranger than we do with ourselves. Do you enjoy your own company? How good are you at meeting your own needs? Spend sometime sitting quietly with yourself and complete the following phrases (the responses maybe shared in your support group):

My favorite color is _____

My favorite flower is _____

My favorite food is _____

My favorite ice cream is _____

My favorite song is _____

My favorite type of music is _____

My favorite movie is _____

My favorite book is _____

My favorite T.V. show is _____

My favorite actress is _____

My favorite actor is _____

My favorite charity is _____

My favorite season is _____

My favorite time of day is _____

My favorite day of the week is _____

My favorite holiday is _____

My favorite animal is _____

My favorite hobby is _____

My favorite restaurant is _____

My favorite vacation spot is _____

My favorite room in my house is _____

My favorite thing about me is _____

If I could do anything as a career, I would _____

If I could travel anyplace in the world it would be _____

If I could live anywhere in the world, it would be _____

Spend a few minutes thinking about your choice of favorite things. What do you think your choices indicate about you?

_____

_____

_____

_____

_____

_____

_____

Exercise #31: *Your Favorite Things*
Collage

SUPPLIES NEEDED:

½ Poster board
5 – 10 Magazines
Scissors
Glue stick
Paper glue

In doing the self-discovery exercise in #30, you were able to list some of your favorite things. In this exercise, you will be able to visualize creatively some of your favorite things.

Collage work is a creative way to provide a visual expression of who you are. What are your favorite things? What pictures represent those goals? A purple flower? A beautiful beach? A bowl of vanilla ice cream? Cut out pictures that represent your favorite things.

- Flip through the magazines and look for pictures or words that visualize your favorite things. If you feel an urge to cut it out—cut it out. It could be a beautiful sunrise, a sumptuous platter of sushi, a cute little Yorkie, an engineer at work, or the Special Olympics. Visualize it! Move closer to yourself by creating a visual representation of your favorite things.

- Do as much cutting as possible in one sitting. You don't have to use every picture that you cut out, but cutting it out gives you the option to use it later.

- Paste the pictures to the cardboard. You may use the glue stick to attach cutouts temporarily until you make a final decision. Again, there is no right or wrong way, enjoy the process. This is your collage allow your creative energy to flow.

- Once your collage is complete, spend a few minutes sitting quietly and meditating on the pictures.

- Allow yourself to feel the joy of being you.

What does each picture mean to you now when you think about it in the context of yourself? Describe some of the pictures you chose and why they are some of your favorite things.

_____

_____

_____

_____

What are the first five (positive) adjectives to come to your mind when you look at the collage? (i.e. bright, peaceful, happy, etc.)

_____

_____

_____

_____

_____

_____

Complete the following in free form (without thinking, write as quickly as you can everything you feel).

I am excited about who I am because

_____

_____

_____

_____

_____

_____

- Leave your collage in a visible place. Whenever you see it, let it be a pleasant reminder of who you are, your wishes, hopes, and dreams.

- Please feel free to share your collage with your group or someone in your support system.

Exercise #32: *Creative Writing*

To Everything a Season…

Our season has come to an end
I've chopped the wood and I've fed the fire
I've hid myself in the bundles of overcoats,
scarves, and gloves
Yet, there was still no warmth to be found
Shivering and shuddering
chilled to the bone
frozen in my own cocoon, focused only on
the darkness
I did not realize spring had come
I only needed to open the window
to see the warmth of the sun
a dared venture outside revealed
the bloom of flowers and the green of grass
And suddenly I realized
To everything a season…
For even after the most brutal winter
life is renewed

This is an example of a poem I wrote, as I was moving through my healing process. Writing is a wonderful way to express feelings. Any expression of feelings is movement towards healing. Be creative. Write a poem or any other short literary expression to express how you are feeling, or to describe where you are at in your healing process. Don't worry if you have never written poetry or don't consider yourself a creative writer. We are all poets. Write your thoughts in short lines, and play with it a little to create a poem. This is an example of changing a sentence into poetry.

This is
an example of
Changing a
Sentence
into
poetry

This
Is
A Poem
Because
I
Said
It is

You don't have to limit your creative juices to poetry. You can write a monologue, a song, a short story, an article, a skit, or whatever you like just be creative. If you are in a support group share your creative writing with the group, if not share it with someone else.

My Poem (Or Other Creative Writing)

_____

_____

_____

_____

_____

_____

_____

_____

_____

_____

_____

_____

_____

_____

Exercise #33: *Mirror Work—Eye to Eye*

Very rarely do we really look at ourselves. Yes, we look in the mirror as we apply makeup or shave but how often do we just stand in a mirror and look into our eyes. Most of us find it uncomfortable after a few seconds. Mirror work is an excellent tool to nurture the relationship with oneself. It is through strengthening the relationship with ourselves that our self-value and self-esteem is developed.

Stand in front of a large mirror and look into your eyes for a moment. Notice if you have the urge to look away. Simply notice it and continue to look into your eyes. After a moment of looking into your eyes, say to yourself, "I love you, I really love you. I am going to nurture you and keep you safe."

As you do this exercise, it is important to pay attention to the feelings and thoughts that come up during the mirror work. Write your thoughts down right away. Do not judge your feelings simply write them down. Spend a few minutes quietly thinking about the experience.

What I feel, when I do this exercise is:

_____

_____

_____

_____

_____

_____

_____

Some nurturing actions I can take to affirm my love for myself is:

_____

_____

_____

_____

_____

_____

_____

Repeat the eye-to-eye mirror work exercise at least twice a day for the next seven days.

Exercise #34: *Mirror Work—Full Body*

In this exercise you will began to connect with your entire body in a loving and nurturing manner. Again, this is an important part of the healing process. Healing emotional wounds requires that we began to develop self-acceptance of our whole selves. Most of us subconsciously reject parts of ourselves on a daily basis. I believe this subconscious rejection impedes the healing process.

Stand in front of a full-length mirror completely undressed. Start with your eyes. Look into your eyes and affirm, "I love you—you are safe." Stare into your eyes for a moment and repeat, "I love you—you are safe." Allow your eyes to slowly look over your face, take in each part of your face. Look at your eyebrows, your eyes, your nose, your lips, and your ears. Pay attention to any thoughts, reactions, or feelings.

Allow your eyes to move slowly down your body taking in each part. Look at your shoulders, your arms, your chest/breast, your abdomen, etc. When you reach your feet allow your eyes to travel slowly back up your body to your eyes taking in each part of your body. Look into your eyes and affirm, "I love you just as you are – You are safe."

Spend a few minutes in quiet reflection paying attention to what comes up. Write your thoughts, feelings, and reactions. Do not sensor the words in anyway, write them exactly as they come up.

What do you feel when you do this exercise?

_____

_____

_____

_____

_____

Did you feel any resistance? If so what?

_____

_____

_____

_____

_____

_____

What was the most difficult part?

_____

_____

_____

_____

_____

_____

What parts of your body did you feel love towards?

_____

_____

_____

_____

_____

What parts of your body did you resist loving?

_____

_____

_____

_____

_____

_____

What can you do to show more love towards the parts of your body you resisted loving?

_____

_____

_____

_____

_____

_____

The full body mirror work should be practiced at least once a day for seven days.

Exercise #35: *Body Image*

How we feel <u>in</u> our body and <u>about</u> our body will affect how we feel about ourselves, how we feel about ourselves will affect how we treat ourselves and how we allow others to treat us. If you have not completed the full body mirror work in exercise #34, please do so before completing this exercise.

1) What parts of your body do you like the most?

I like my _____ because _____

I like my _____ because _____

I like my _____ because _____

I like my _____ because _____

I like my _____ because _____

I like my _____ because _____

I like my _____ because _____

2) What part(s) of your body do you cover up or camouflage (ladies this includes <u>needing</u> to wear make up). Maybe you are comfortable in clothing, but there are parts of you that you are uncomfortable with when you are undressed.

I am uncomfortable with my _____ because _____

_____

I am uncomfortable with my _____ because _____

_____

I am uncomfortable with my _____ because _____

_____

I am uncomfortable with my _____ because _____

_____

Pay attention to those parts of you that you are not okay with and the reason why. Are your expectations based on external reasons or are they unrealistic? Such as gaining the acceptance/affection of someone, or wanting the body of a nineteen year old at age fifty, or wanting to be four inches taller. Are there some areas that can be improved through proper diet, exercise, grooming, etc?

Self-love is self-acceptance. Self-acceptance is accepting our body—just as it is now!!! Love yourself now and you will intuitively create the changes needed to feel better in and about your body. For each part of your body you are uncomfortable with complete the following statements. Challenge yourself to think of at least one positive attribute for each body part. (i.e. I appreciate my feet because they take me places)

I appreciate my _____ because _____

I appreciate my _____ because _____

I appreciate my _____ because _____

I appreciate my _____ because _____

I appreciate my _____ because _____

I appreciate my _____ because _____

I appreciate my _____ because _____

I appreciate my _____ because _____

Repeat these positive statements at least three times a day for the next seven days. If you think of other positive attributes add them to the list!!

Exercise #36: *Body Nurturing*

How well do you take care of your body? Do you feed it nourishing foods? Are you getting enough rest? Do you get enough exercise? Do you lovingly groom your body? Do you have medical issues that need your attention? When we are healing from the hurt of a relationship, it can be easy to neglect our body care. However, taking care of your body is absolutely necessary in the healing of your emotions (it is all connected).

Think about this—when you are hurting from the pain of a relationship there are so many factors out of your control, including our own emotions at times and this creates a sense of powerlessness. Regardless, we do have control over how we care for our body. Taking good care of our body gives us a sense of empowerment, boost our self-esteem, and help us heal when relationships hurt.

Make realistic commitments to nurturing your body in the following ways:

• I commit to eating better by (be specific, i.e. reduce/eliminate sugar, coffee, fried foods, white flour, junk foods, red meats, dairy products, etc.):

_____

_____

_____

_____

_____

• I will drink more water each day by drinking at least ___ ounces of water. (It is recommended that we drink at least half our body weight in ounces each day).

• I will take the following vitamins and/or nutritional supplements:

_____

_____

_____

_____

_____

- I will get _____ hours of sleep every night (set an alarm clock to go to bed).

- I will improve my quality of sleep by (i.e. journaling before bed, reading positive literature, meditation, relaxing music, aromatherapy: avoid dramatic T.V., movies, news, newspapers and books).

_____

_____

_____

_____

_____

- I will exercise _____ minutes _____ times per week. I will do the following exercise(s) on the following days:

_____

_____

_____

_____

_____

- I will read the following information on health, fitness, and nutrition (i.e. books, magazines, articles, and websites). Your local health food store often provides free literature on nutrition and health.

_____

_____

_____

_____

• I will commit to the following grooming routines (i.e. haircuts, manicures, pedicures, shaves, massages, waxing, electrolysis, etc.):

<u>Grooming</u>   <u>How often (put it on the calendar)</u>

_____   _____

_____   _____

_____   _____

_____   _____

_____   _____

_____   _____

• I will take care of the following health issue(s), (include dental and eye care (make appointments):

_____ by _____ (date)

_____ by _____ (date)

_____ by _____ (date)

_____ by _____ (date)

_____ by _____ (date)

• I will eliminate the following destructive habits (i.e. smoking, excessive drinking, drug use, etc.)

_____ by _____ (date)

_____ by _____ (date)

_____ by _____ (date)

_____ by _____ (date)

• I will seek help in eliminating the above habit(s) from:

_____

_____

_____

_____

_____

• I will share my commitment to nurture my body with:

_____

_____

_____

_____

_____

Exercise #37: *Your Beliefs About Sex*

This exercise deals with examining your belief system about sex. Our emotional programming and belief system around sex will determine our current attitudes toward sex. Understanding what our subconscious beliefs are will help is to confront and change outdated belief systems. Remember what we believe at our deepest level internally will manifest in our lives externally.

If you are in a support group, you may do this exercise in your group or as a homework assignment and share your feelings about it with your group. Often if we think we are going to share our response, there will be a natural tendency to filter our thoughts. If you are doing group work, make an agreement with the other group members to share only your thoughts and feelings about the exercise—not what you write. This will create a safer environment and allow for more honest venting in the free form writing. Wherever you choose to do this exercise, it is important that you do not change or edit what you wrote when you are done. The only person you have to share it with is you. Remember, the first thoughts that come to your mind is very important and can give you a lot of insight into yourself.

For each of the following phrases write for three to five minutes every thought that comes to your mind.

The messages I received from my parents about sex were:

_____

_____

_____

_____

_____

The messages I received from others (church, school, community) as a child about sex were:

_____

_____

_____

_____

My personal experiences with sex have taught me:

_____

_____

_____

_____

_____

Some decisions I have made about sex are:

_____

_____

_____

_____

_____

- Re-read your response without judgment. Don't be surprised if you responded with some thoughts or beliefs that you were not even aware you believed in. It is okay, journal about your reaction.

- What beliefs do you feel no longer serve your highest purpose? Would you like to move beyond those outdated beliefs? If so, draw a line through those beliefs you are eliminating.

- What beliefs would you like to nurture? Circle those.

- Think about what you wrote for a few days and re-visit your response, does your reaction to your response seem to change?

- Allow a few days to pass and re-do the exercise. Write for three to five minutes every thought that comes to you mind.

What I believe about sex is:

_____

_____

_____

_____

Is there any difference? If so, what?

_____

_____

_____

_____

_____

Why do you think this is so?

_____

_____

_____

_____

Again, draw a line through the beliefs you would like to eliminate. Circle those beliefs you would like to nurture.

What I would like my future experiences with sex to be are:

_____

_____

_____

_____

_____

Exercise #38: *Love or Lust?*

Sexual energy is a very powerful element of the human condition and sexual attraction can be so powerful that many of us mistake it for love. It is clear by today's advertising that marketing executives recognize the power of sex. Everything from beer, to cars, to toothpaste advertisements has strong sexual overtones. I believe as result of the negative messages we receive from the media and other examples we have as a society become desensitized to sexual innuendos. Because of this desensitization, we may sexualize our emotions or at the other extreme, we emotionalize our sex. In other words, we may use sex to escape from our feelings or we may think we are in love when it is really only about good sex.

It is important as we move through our healing process that we begin to understand how to differentiate between mishandled sexual energy that creates compulsive and/or unhealthy sexual behaviors, and conscious sexual expressions that enhance rather than harm.

The following statements are indicators of mishandled sexual energy. Please respond to the statements based on all of your collective sexual experiences by circling true or false.

- If I feel a strong sexual attraction towards someone, I am compelled to pursue the relationship.

True False

- I have used sex as a means of manipulation and/or control.

True False

- I have felt shame as a result of my sexual activity.

True False

- I feel incomplete when I am not involved in a sexual relationship.

True False

- I have become sexually involved with people without knowing them.

True False

- I have engaged in emotionless sex—devoid of any attachment to my partner.

True False

- I have felt obligated to have sex, even when I did not want to.

True False

• I have stayed in painful/unhealthy relationships because the sex was good.

True False

• I have obsessively fantasized about sex.

True False

• I have been involved in more than one sexual relationship at the same time.

True False

• I have been abused sexually.

True False

• I have been sexually abusive.

True False

• I have confused sexual attractions with love.

True False

Review your responses to the previous statements. Did you circle yes to any statement?

What feelings do you have about the statements that were true for you?

_____

_____

_____

The following statements are indicators of healthy sexual expressions. Please respond true or false to the statement based on your overall sexual experiences. Although some statements may not have related to your sexual experiences in the past, the good news is you can work towards making these statements your truth in the future.

• I engage in sex that nurtures and enhance my relationship.

True False

• I set healthy sexual boundaries.

True False

• I have sex as a byproduct of my healthy relationships.

True False

• I feel intimate and connected towards my partner during sex.

True False

• I consistently practice sexual monogamy.

True False

• I openly discuss my sexual needs with my partner.

True False

• I practice mutually consensual sex.

True False

• I recognized the difference between sexual attraction and emotional attachment.

True False

• I feel safe and secure during sex.

True False

• I honor my partner's sexual needs. True False

• I am comfortable with myself outside of a relationship.

True False

• I develop intimacy in my relationships before becoming sexually involved.

True False

What feelings do you have about the statements that were false for you?

_____

_____

_____

What can you do in the future to make these statements your truth?

_____

_____

_____

Exercise #39: *Healthy Sexuality*

Our sexuality is more than our sexual identity or our sexual orientation. Our sexuality affects every area of our life. It is the first tag bestowed upon us at birth and we respond to the world through the eyes of our sexuality. Our sexuality integrates our bodies with the rest of the world. We develop a perception of ourselves based on this integration and the cultural influences of our society. If we feel positive about our sexuality, we will respond to the world from a sense of security that accompanies a healthy self-esteem or sense of self-worth. When we have an unhealthy sense of sexuality, we may respond to the world from a place of shame and/ or guilt. This shame or guilt may taint many of our views and lower our self-esteem.

The way that I feel about my sexuality is:

_____

_____

_____

_____

_____

_____

_____

_____

List any thoughts/beliefs you have about your sexuality that you feel are no longer conducive to a healthy sense of self-worth.

_____

_____

_____

_____

_____

_____

_____

Are you willing to let go of those thoughts/beliefs/actions? If yes, review what you have written and completely blackout any thoughts/beliefs/actions that you would like to eliminate.

What life affirming thoughts/beliefs/action can you use to replace the negative thought/

beliefs/ actions?

_____

_____

_____

_____

_____

_____

_____

_____

Exercise #40: *Using Your Creative Energy*

Creating something where there is nothing is very healing. It is empowering to see an activity from beginning to end with a tangible result. When relationships hurt and dissolve it is a painful ending. Arts and crafts give us an opportunity to have a happy ending. It is also an excellent way to channel frustration and excess sexual energy.

What arts and crafts do you enjoy? You don't have to be an expert or have a lot of practice at anything. There are literally hundreds of arts and crafts with easy to follow directions that even a ten year old could follow. It is not important what it is you do, rather the important thing is to do something! The only suggestion is that it should be something that could be done in one to two weeks. Avoid long drawn out projects as this could lead to frustration and further add to your stress.

If you have a creative hobby renew it. Create something for yourself first then if you are inspired create something to give as a gift. Some ideas are:

Jewelry, key tags, latch hook, curtains or pillows, make or decorate candles, build something such as toolbox, birdhouse, doghouse, chest, etc., decorate boxes, gift bags, t-shirts, or flower pots.

If you don't have a hobby go to your local arts and crafts store or even your local discount department store and take a look around. Spend a few minutes slowly walking up and down the aisles of the craft section. Select something simple and easy, it should be relaxing and fun to do, otherwise you might get frustrated and not complete the project. It is very important that you complete the project. If you are doing group work, make a commitment to your group or to someone in your support system. You can even do the arts and craft as part of the group or with someone else. This will help keep you motivated.

I will use my creative energy to create _____ for myself.

I will use my creative energy to create _____ for _____

Remember to journal any feelings/reactions you may have to this process. Was it difficult for you to get started, to finish? How does it feel to create something?

_____

_____

_____

_____

Exercise #41: *Harmonious Living*

Harmony in our home environment or the lack thereof is a direct result of our emotional selves. Harmony is a result of right order, organization, and unity. These elements maybe absent from our lives on many levels when we are hurting from a relationship. I believe our home gives many clues as to what is going within our psyche; therefore, it is important to pay attention to the areas of disharmony.

While going through my healing process, I recognized disorder in my life when I walked into my kitchen, my bedroom, or bathroom. I literally felt shame at the thought of letting anyone into these rooms. I also realized this disorder was a form of protection—it kept me from letting people too close to me, especially the opposite sex. During an especially difficult period in my process, I found myself having a difficult time setting boundaries with someone I was attracted to but intuitively knew getting involved with him would not serve my highest good. When he called to ask if he could come by, I thought about what disorder my bedroom was in and I was able to say no. It was then I realized that I used my chaos as a defense mechanism, it was literally a barrier, and it kept me separate and alone. While I disliked the disorder, subconsciously I continued to create it. The rooms in my home are very symbolic and represent my different dimensions. Therefore, the disorder in these rooms is symbolic as well.

Sometimes there is disorder right at my front door—when my son drops his book bags, basketball, shoes, or whatever right in the foyer. I may leave my workbag, shoes, or whatever in the foyer also. When there is a lot of clutter in my foyer, I do not want to open my front door to anyone, except maybe for my sister, with whom I feel very safe. If I have an unexpected visitor, I feel a twinge of shame and fear of judgment. I feel my foyer represents my physical dimension– my physical appearance. Maybe I need a manicure or pedicure, or maybe my hair needs washing, I'm wearing old sweats or I just feel bloated. When I feel my physical appearance is not at its best I may feel self-conscious and withdraw if I happen to be caught off guard.

My living room and dining room represents my business and social side. My living room is usually always clean and presentable—ready to receive guests if they get past the foyer. This is where I entertain—the part I show to the world. I am entertaining, funny, and intellectual in these rooms. They are safe and there is always an element of harmony. They show off my creativeness—my good taste. I feel beautiful, I feel strong, and successful in these rooms. I spend very little time alone in these rooms—they are social rooms.

My kitchen represents my more vulnerable and more emotional side. I sit in there with those people I feel closest to and with whom I feel familiar. Mostly family members and close friends I welcome into this room. I am emotionally vulnerable in this room. A lot of insight about my personality is in my kitchen. There is usually always some clutter, but most of the clutter feels acceptable—there is no shame attached to it. I feel very comfortable in my kitchen and if I am not feeling very comfortable with someone, they are not invited into my kitchen, but I will sit with them in the dining room or maybe the living room. I let my guard down in my kitchen. I talk, I share, I listen, I laugh, I cry, I cook, I serve, I create, I nourish, I bond, there is much love in my kitchen. In a way, my kitchen represents my heart, because I love to feed people and will serve everyone from my kitchen (heart) but not everyone is welcomed in.

The upstairs rooms represent family and are very personal—off limits to the world. The stairs leading to it can be seen from the front door, but those rooms are private—not public domain. The guest room is on the second floor and tends to be a gathering place for everything in the house where there is nowhere else to put stuff. It is full of clutter, but it does not feel chaotic. I usually prepare for guest by doing a special cleaning and accommodations are made. Otherwise, I allow my son to have his space and I don't give much thought to what people think or feel about our personal family rooms. We have a lot of joy and happiness, there is harmony and peace, but it is personal. I feel a lot of peace when I am in my son's room and I will often go there just to look around when I really need to be centered. I am always filled with gratitude when I spend time in his room.

My prayer room represents the spiritual side of me. I find it interesting how it is on display to the world (it sits right off my living room) yet it is off limits to the all. It is a place where I commune and connect with God, and while the world can see the visible proof of my spirituality and I express the beauty of it (I love the aesthetics of my prayer room), it is my sacred place for God and I. This room is very harmonious.

The rooms that create the most anxiety, shame, and fear are my bedroom and my personal bathroom. These rooms represent my psychological side, which include my sexual stuff. There were times in my bathroom when I felt dirty and a sense of shame. My shower was not cleaned, neither was the sink or the toilet. The paradox is the bathroom also represents a place of cleansing, of waste removal, of washing away both literally and figuratively. I think the bathroom inside my bedroom represents the deepest level of my sexual self. Of course, these rooms are not open to the public and only those I am very intimate with ever enter. It is my deepest psychological self.

I have beautiful furnishings and décor and these rooms are very beautiful when they are clean and tidy. I feel happy, peaceful, and secure when I walk into these rooms—safe, content, even inspired when I wake up to a clean suite of rooms. I feel clean and refreshed when I shower and dress in a clean bathroom. When I come home at the end of the day and walk into a made up bed and a clean bedroom, I feel good about my life and myself. When those rooms are messy, I just want to close the door on it and spend the least amount of time there as possible. It is the same if I am overwhelmed or dealing with an uncomfortable issue, I can shut down and deal with everything but that issue, and if I get even a remote reminder of it, I feel shame or guilt. My bedroom suite represents all my hopes and my dreams, my hurts, my grief, my unresolved issues, my guilt, my debts, my resentments, and my fears. Nevertheless, it also represents my potential, my creativity, my inspiration, my place of rest, my healing, my nurturing, and my purpose. Within my psyche are many things that at times may become jumbled up and disorganized, it represents disharmony. However, when it is organized and ordered I feel peace, joy, and so much love in these rooms.

If your home is symbolic of who you are…which rooms in your home represent the following dimensions, and why do you think it is so?

Your Physical Self:

_____

_____

_____

_____

Your Social Self:

_____

_____

_____

_____

Your Psychological Self:

_____

_____

_____

_____

Your Spiritual Self:

_____

_____

_____

_____

Which room(s) in your home do you find the most comfort, and why do you think this

is so?

_____

_____

_____

_____

_____

_____

_____

What can you do to create a more harmonious environment in the rooms you find the

least comfort? (i.e. paint the room, redecorate, organize, etc.)

_____

_____

_____

_____

_____

_____

_____

Exercise #42: *Remove the Clutter*

Just as we discussed in the previous chapter clutter in our surroundings is indicative of mental clutter. However, the reverse is also true if we clear up the physical clutter it will help create mental/emotional clarity. When relationships hurt, it is easy to neglect our surroundings. However, as we move through the hurt it is important to clear up the clutter along the way.

The first step is to identify the clutter in your life. It could be everywhere or in just one room. Maybe it is in the backseat of your car or the three hundred receipts in your wallet. Is it the junk mail piled on the kitchen counter or a drawer in your bedroom? Clutter owns pieces of us and it chips away at our self-esteem. Do you feel a twinge of guilt every time you see the clutter? That twinge is a direct assault on your self-esteem. On the other hand, have you become numb to the clutter? The numbness is an indirect assault on your self-esteem.

Clutter is often an indication of holding on to old stuff. Let it go! Letting go of the old creates room for the new. What pieces of your past are you still holding onto? Clothes, jewelry, old greeting cards, pictures, or movie stubs? A wise woman once said to me, "God cannot place something new in your hand if it is full of old stuff." Let it go which will create room for new experiences and while you're at it, rid yourself of the other clutter too.

I see clutter showing up in my life in the following area(s):

_____

_____

_____

_____

_____

I have been holding onto the following (clutter) from my past:

_____

_____

_____

_____

_____

The reason(s) I have been holding on is:

_____

_____

_____

_____

I am willing to get rid of the following clutter:

_____

_____

_____

_____

_____

- Spend the next few days clearing up the clutter—one space at a time.

- Start with the smallest project, (like your wallet) and complete one project before moving to the next.

- Set a date for the larger projects like cleaning out the garage or spare room. Put it on your calendar

- If you have not worn it in a year or used it in six months, you probably won't miss it.

- As you discard each piece of clutter, consciously affirm, *"I release the old to make room for the new."*

- Journal about any feelings or reactions you may have.

Exercise # 43: *Acts of Service*

If not for my involvement in community service, I am certain I would not have survived those dark days of emotional pain. However, being involved in a variety of service activities and having commitments, gave me an opportunity to focus outside of my issues and myself. I was able to realize my purpose through my service work. Helping to make the lives of others better gave me faith in the healing process of life. I personally feel that it is part of our divine purpose to make our piece of the world better than the way we find it.

One of the best ways to feel good about yourself is to be of service to others. Service work or acts of kindness are very healing because it creates in us a spirit of connectedness to others. It also boosts our self-esteem and self-confidence to be a part of bringing joy, comfort, or support to others. The natural laws of reaping and sowing apply in every area of our lives. What we put out determines what comes back. If we sow caring, love, and support that is what we will get in return in many, many ways.

Service work is any act of kindness that we do without expectation of reward. A major act of service would be helping to build a house for a homeless family. However smaller acts of service such as giving a compliment to a stranger at the bus stop, or picking up a gum wrapper off the sidewalk are important acts of service that we should practice on a daily basis. Imagine spending your life looking for opportunities to do acts of service. The joy will come back to you and help heal your heart when relationships hurt.

- Over the next seven days practice cultivating a spirit of service.

- On each day, commit to doing at least three random acts of service.

- At the end of the day, log your acts of service in the service log.

RANDOM ACTS OF SERVICE

Examples: Pick up litter, let someone out in traffic, give up your seat on the bus, offer a compliment to a stranger, etc.

Day 1 _____

Day 2 _____

Day 3 _____

Day 4 _____

Day 5 _____

Day 6 _____

Day 7 _____

• Make a commitment to take on a planned act of service. (There are hundreds of opportunities awaiting you right now in your community. What cause is close to your heart? A walk for cancer or AIDS? Community clean up? Church or civic organization fundraiser? Outreach to the homeless or battered women shelter? PTA/school volunteer or little league coach? The list goes on and on.)

I will commit to (planned act of service) _____ by (date) _____.

I will commit to (planned act of service) _____ by (date) _____.

I am willing to commit _____ hours per month participating in a planned act of service.

After seven days write your thoughts on, "How does it feel to show kindness/love?"

_____

_____

_____

_____

_____

_____

_____

_____

Continue to practice acts of kindness on daily basis.

Exercise #44: *Self Definition*

One of the issues I had in relationships was I became whomever I thought the person I was with wanted me to be. As the fifth born out of nine children, I was a typical middle child without any clear definition. Along with all my siblings there was always, "extra" people living with us so there was no such thing as personal space. Very early in life I literally became the, "middle man" as I assumed the role of advocate for my younger siblings. I became very co-dependent and defined myself by the needs of others, becoming who other people thought I was. My healing process gave me the opportunity to define clearly my personal boundaries.

How do you define yourself? Is it by the work that you do? Do you define yourself by the way others define you? Kujichagulia is a Swahili term that means self-definition. The principle of kujichagulia is to define you for yourself and to refuse to be defined by others. This is an important principle to embody in the healing process because when we define ourselves by our own internal definitions rather than our external circumstances then we are continually empowered to re-create ourselves anew everyday!

Put your name in the center of the heart on the following page. In the space around the heart, answer the following questions.

#1 What are six definitions that others would use to describe you? (ex. Student, nurse)

#2 What are six definitions that you would use to describe yourself?

#3 What are six adjectives that you feel best describe you? (ex. smart, funny, moody)

#4 How do you describe your race/ethnicity?

#5 What culture or subculture do you consider yourself a member of? (ex. law enforcement, artist, religion, vegetarian)

#6 What are six values you believe in most strongly? (i.e. spirituality, family, health)

#7 What do you do on a daily basis that reflects your most important value?

#1 How others describe you   #2. Self description

_____   _____
_____   _____
_____   _____
_____   _____
_____   _____

#3 Adjectives

_____
_____
_____
_____
_____

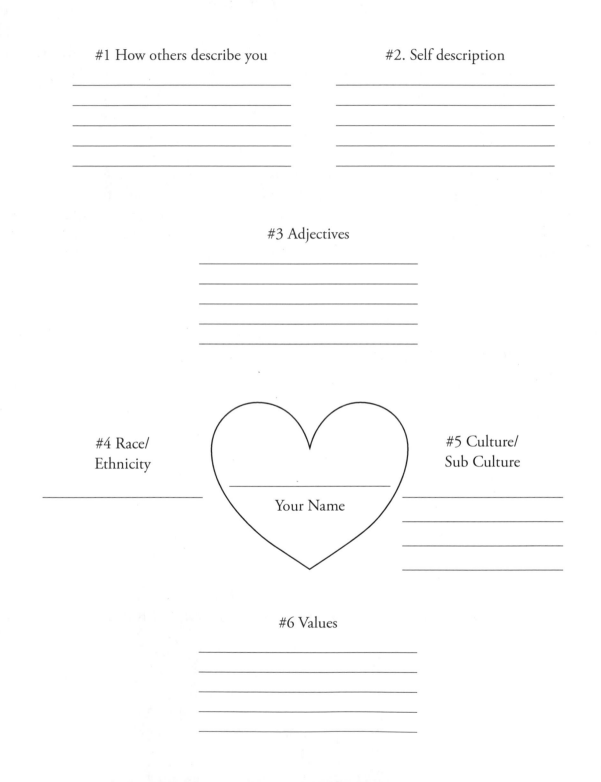

#4 Race/
Ethnicity   Your Name   #5 Culture/
                                                          Sub Culture

_____   _____
                                                          _____
                                                          _____
                                                          _____

#6 Values

_____
_____
_____
_____
_____

Exercise #45: *Leisure Activities*

Developing healthy leisure skills is an important part of the healing process when relationships hurt. Often times our social lives have become so intertwined with that of our REMY! we may find ourselves at a loss with what to do with our time. Boredom can lead to increased anxiety as we struggle with the myriad of feelings left by the void and loneliness when relationships hurt.

It is important that we have constructive ways of spending our leisure time. This exercise will help you construct a list of leisure activities that you could easily do when you find yourself feeling bored or restless. Balance this list to include a variety of things you could do alone at home as well social activities. If you have children or pets, include activities you could do with them as well.

Some examples of leisure activities may include:

- Join a sports team

- Take a dance class

- Go window shopping (leave the checkbook and credit cards home)

- Do yard work

- Read a book (avoid romance novels)

- Go to a theme park—ride the roller coasters —scream your head off

- Go to the beach

- Rebuild motorcycles or just go for a ride on one

- Go to your favorite fishing hole

- Paint a room in your house

- Learn a foreign language

- Plant a garden

Think about who you are. What activities do you enjoy? What activities are you interested in? What activities would you like to learn? List as many as come to mind and spend the next week developing your list, adding things as they come to mind. Remember, the list should be things that you could easily do without much planning or expense.

---

[1]Relationship Evaluation Mechanism for Your Information, or the person you were/are in a relationship with.

1. _____   27. _____

2. _____   28. _____

3. _____   29. _____

4. _____   30. _____

5. _____   31. _____

6. _____   32. _____

7. _____   33. _____

8. _____   34. _____

9. _____   35. _____

10. _____   36. _____

11. _____   37. _____

12. _____   38. _____

13. _____   39. _____

14. _____   40. _____

15. _____   41. _____

16. _____   42. _____

17. _____   43. _____

18. _____   44. _____

19. _____   45. _____

20. _____   46. _____

21. _____   47. _____

22. _____   48. _____

23. _____   49. _____

24. _____   50. _____

25. _____   51. _____

26. _____   52. _____

Exercise #46: *Set Realistic Goals*

Where do you see yourself in six months? What about next year this time or five years from now? Are you just going through each day only to wake up and go through the next one or does your life have purpose with clear goals.

After struggling through the healing process when relationships hurt, it is important to find purpose in our lives. Having clear and tangible goals and working towards those goals helps to give our lives a sense of purpose. Some keys to remember when setting goals are:

- Make them measurable. 'I will save money,' is not measurable. However, 'I will save $3,000 in one year,' is measurable.

- Make them specific. 'I will feel better about myself' is not specific. However, 'I will lose ten pounds,' is more specific.

- Make them attainable. 'I will be a neurosurgeon in one year is probably not attainable to most of us. However, 'I will graduate from college in five years,' is attainable.

- Always set a reasonable timeframe for accomplishing your goals. A reasonable timeframe for short-term goals are three to nine months, and one to five years for long-terms goals.

Using the following chart, develop both short and long-term goals. Make sure they are measurable, tangible, and attainable within the time frame you choose.

Today's Date: _____

Goals	Time Frame	Goals	Time Frame
SPIRITUAL		**FAMILY**	
_____	_____	_____	_____
_____	_____	_____	_____
_____	_____	_____	_____
_____	_____	_____	_____

Goals	Time Frame	Goals	Time Frame
CAREER		**EDUCATIONAL**	
_____	___	_____	___
_____	___	_____	___
_____	___	_____	___
_____	___	_____	___
SPIRITUAL		**FAMILY**	
_____	___	_____	___
_____	___	_____	___
_____	___	_____	___
_____	___	_____	___
HEALTH/FITNESS		**TRAVEL**	
_____	___	_____	___
_____	___	_____	___
_____	___	_____	___
_____	___	_____	___
PERSONAL		**FINANCIAL**	
_____	___	_____	___
_____	___	_____	___
_____	___	_____	___
_____	___	_____	___
EMOTIONAL		**HOME**	
_____	___	_____	___
_____	___	_____	___
_____	___	_____	___
_____	___	_____	___
OTHER		**OTHER**	
_____	___	_____	___
_____	___	_____	___
_____	___	_____	___
_____	___	_____	___

What changes do you need to make in your life in order to reach your goals?

_____

_____

_____

_____

_____

_____

_____

What goals can you set to attain over the next seven days? Examples: clean out garage, complete a project, make specific phone calls, exercise four times during the week; attend a religious service. Name at least seven.

_____

_____

_____

_____

_____

_____

_____

After seven days, review your goals. Were you able to accomplish your goals? If not, why?

_____

_____

_____

_____

What do you need to do to make these goals a reality in your life?

_____

_____

_____

_____

_____

Are you willing to re-commit:

Exercise #47: *Visualize Your Future*
Creating a Collage

SUPPLIES NEEDED:

½ Poster board
5 – 10 Magazines
Scissors
Glue stick
Paper glue

If you have not done the goal setting in exercise #46 it is strongly suggested that you do so before beginning this exercise.

Collage work is a creative way to provide a visual expression of your future. What are your personal goals? Visualize your future using the personal goals you set in exercise #46. What pictures represent those goals? A happy family? A graduate? A marathon runner? Cut out pictures that represent your goals.

- Flip through the magazines and look for pictures or words that visualize your goals. If you feel an urge to cut it out—cut it out. It could be an exercise class, a brand new Mercedes, a healthy salad, an exotic beach, or a beautiful home. You may also choose words, some words I chose were laughter, serenity, no-clutter, and celebration. Go ahead imagine it! Move closer to creating your future by creating a visual representation of your goal.

- Cut out as many pictures as possible in one sitting. You don't have to use every picture that you cut out, but cutting it out gives you the option to use it later.

- Paste the pictures to the cardboard. You may use the glue stick to attach cutouts temporarily until you make a final decision. Again, there is no right or wrong way, enjoy the process. This is your creation, allow your creative energy to flow and have fun in the process imagining your future as bright and cheerful.

Once your collage is complete, spend a few minutes sitting quietly and meditating on the pictures. Describe what each picture means to you now when you think about it in the context of your future?

_____

_____

_____

_____

_____

_____

_____

How attainable are the goals represented in the pictures? Allow yourself to feel the joy of possibilities.

List four positive adjectives that come to mind when you look at your collage. (i.e. prosperous, healthy, successful, etc.)

_____   _____

_____   _____

Write the adjectives on post it notes and post them in visible locations. Whenever you see them remind yourself that, you can have your future now!

Complete the following in free form (without thinking, write as quickly as you can every thought that comes to your mind)

I am excited about my future because

_____

_____

_____

_____

_____

_____

- Leave your collage in a visible place. Whenever you see it, let it be a visible reminder of your goals.

- Please feel free to share your collage with your group or someone in your support system.

Exercise #48: *Relapse Prevention*

Even after a period of separation and healing work, there maybe a tendency to return to painful, destructive, or unhealthy relationships. The temptation or thoughts of returning to the relationship or spending time in the company of your REMY! are a normal part of your healing process.

It has been said, that insanity is repeating the same thing and expecting different results. That being said, how much sense does it make to return to the same person, with the same issues and expect the relationship to be different this time? However, we hope against hope, rationalize, and justify our decisions to return.

As an addictions counselor, I have worked with thousands of men and women who returned to the painful destructive lifestyle of substance abuse despite the havoc their addiction may have caused them and their family. Part of what happens in these relapses is that they forget the pain, they may have selective memory- only focusing on the good times, or they may minimize the pain, telling themselves it really wasn't that bad. However, before the actual relapse happens, there are always warning signs that if you heed and deal with the warning signs you could prevent the relapse from occurring.

This same process applies in relationship relapse. The relapse does not happen when we find ourselves with our REMY, but long before we return to the painful relationship. Relapse is a process and it begins in our spirit and our thoughts. Your ex maybe very apologetic or manipulative and you temporarily forget the pain of the relationship. You may have a strong sexual attraction or you are lonely and your ex's presence is familiar and in ways comforting. There maybe extenuating circumstances such as children or finances.

The following are some possible warning signs and suggested interventions to help prevent relationship relapse:

<u>Warning Signs</u>

- Thinking of your REMY with selective thinking, remembering only the good and contemplating returning to the relationship.

- Feeling financial pressures.

- Feeling guilty about the children.

- Feeling responsible for you REMY"s feelings

- Feeling strong jealousy at the thought of your REMY being with someone else.

<u>R</u>elationship <u>E</u>valuation <u>M</u>echanism for <u>Y</u>our Information, or the person you were/are in a relationship with.

Interventions:

- Share honestly with your support system without judging your feelings. (Remember feelings are not necessarily facts and you do not have to act on everything you feel.)

- Use your caller ID. Personalize the caller ID on your cell and home phone if possible to warn you when your ex calls. Some tags to use are: warning, danger, do not answer, do not call, pray, more misery, heartache, drama, or REMY. Do not accept calls from unknown numbers.

- Avoid places where you know your ex is likely to be. If you must go, take support or stay in touch with support system by cell phone.

- Don't listen to music that reminds you of your ex. Change the radio station or listen to classic music, jazz, or spiritually uplifting music.

- Let go of the clothing, jewelry, or other items you wear that were given to you by your ex. These items create soul ties (emotional connections). You are more apt to relapse if you have a constant reminder of your ex.

- Complete the pro and cons list. List all possible reasons for returning to and staying out of the relationship. List everything that comes to your mind no matter how trivial it may seem. (i.e. she makes great meat loaf or his feet are rough and scratchy.)

REASONS TO LET GO   REASONS TO HOLD ON

_____   _____

_____   _____

_____   _____

_____   _____

_____   _____

_____   _____

_____   _____

_____   _____

_____   _____

_____   _____

_____   _____

_____   _____

_____   _____

_____   _____

_____   _____

_____   _____

_____   _____

- Examine this list—does one side out weight the other? Write your thoughts and feeling about this exercise.

- Write some of your reasons to let go on sticky notes. Place the sticky notes in visible locations to remind you of your choice to let go. The phone is a perfect place to place a sticky note.

- Re-read your journal and review completed exercises in this book to remind you of what you have gone through and the progress you have made.

- Get professional help! Seek the advice of a lawyer, financial advisor, individual counseling, or any other professional that could assist you with your specific situation.

- PRAY! Don't minimize the power of prayer. PUSH—<u>P</u>ray <u>U</u>ntil <u>S</u>omething <u>H</u>appens!

Exercise #49: *Relationship Compatibility*

I still shudder when I think about the first person I dated after my marriage ended. He smoked like a chimney and cursed like a sailor (two habits I simply do not care for). He was from a very different cultural background with very different values and beliefs. In fact, when I look back, we were not compatible at all! Yet, at the time, I was very excited and convinced myself of the possibility of having a real relationship with this man. The bottom line was I was lonely, afraid, hurting and wanted someone to make me feel good. It only took a few weeks for the glitter to wear off and for me to see how ridiculous the idea of a relationship with this man was. It was then that I made a conscious decision to stay out of any relationship until I spent time healing myself and defining what I want in a relationship.

Sometimes when we have been hurt in a relationship, there is tendency to latch onto the first person that shows us attention or makes us feel good. This is dangerous because all relationships feel good in the beginning. We are involved with each other's representative the first few months of a new relationship, seeing only the best side of the person. This is often referred to as the honeymoon phase of the relationship. We are on our best behavior representing all of our positive qualities and we only want to see the best qualities in the other person. Generally, people will show us who they are but we may become so busy entertaining our own fantasy of who we want them to be that we don't pay attention to the warnings signs. There is often a great deal of denial in the initial stages of relationships. However, if we have prepared a relationship compatibility list we have a frame of reference from which to work and we decrease our chances of going on that trip down the river denial. If we do happen to float away, the relationship compatibility list can be the guide to help us find our way back.

I often tell my clients, "If you don't make a choice, you don't have a choice." When it comes to whom we will date, spend time with, or have a relationship with, we do have a choice. However, we often forfeit this choice by being attracted to someone simply because the someone is attracted to us. We maybe very clear about what we are attracted to in terms of physical appearance or profession, but may not have a clue as to what other traits a potential partner may need to complete the package. In this exercise, you will develop a relationship compatibility list to help you select potential partners. Keep in mind that chances are very slim that anyone will possess every trait that you list, but this will give you a working understanding of what it is you are looking for and help save you time and energy.

Some areas to focus on for compatibility are physical, social, emotional, spiritual, cultural, financial, sexual, education/intellectual, and hobbies/interest. As you begin to think about the traits you would like in a potential partner, remember we attract who we are. Therefore, think about who you are now as you begin to think about the traits you would want in a potential partner. Complete the following exercise, taking as much time as you need. When I did my relationship compatibility, it took me several weeks as I continued to review and add to it. The first column is merely examples of the trait. Please feel free to use your own definitions to personalize the trait.

Characteristics/Traits	List the characteristics/traits you currently possess	List the characteristics/ traits you would like in your mate
Physical • Appearance • Hygiene/grooming • Physically fit • Health conscious • Clothing style • Eating habits		
Social: • Family oriented • Outgoing • Laid back • Charming • Party Animal • Proactive takes initiative • Dependable • Organized • Humorous		

Characteristics/Traits	List the characteristics/traits you currently possess	List the characteristics/traits you would like in your mate
Spiritual • Believes in God • Practice prayer/meditation • Has conviction in beliefs • Reads spiritual literature • Attends services • Fellowship with others		
Cultural • Values • Beliefs • Holidays • Celebrations • Food • Music		

Characteristics/Traits	List the characteristics/traits you currently possess	List the characteristics/traits you would like in your mate
Financial/Occupation • Stability • Responsible • Work Ethics • Successful • Has established goals • Pays bills/obligationss		
Sexual • Passionate • Likes to kiss • Pillow talk • Erotic • Romantic • Sensitive		

Characteristics/Traits	List the characteristics/traits you currently possess	List the characteristics/traits you would like in your mate
Educational/Intellectual • Education level • Well read • Open to learning • Articulate • Stimulating conversation		
Hobbies/Interests • Travel • Pets • Sports • Performing arts • Movies/theater • Volunteer work		

Review your relationship compatibility.

- Are the characteristics you would like in your mate compatible to the characteristics you currently possess?

- If you do not currently possess the characteristics you seek in a mate, are you willing to become what you want? What changes are you willing to make?

_____

_____

_____

_____

_____

_____

_____

• Are you willing to set boundaries based on what you are looking for in a relationship? What characteristics are you not willing to compromise?

_____

_____

_____

_____

_____

_____

Exercise #50: *Relationship Creed*

If you have done the prior assignment, you should have a good idea of the characteristics you are looking for in a partner. Equally, it is important that you are clear about what your expectations are from the relationship. This involves not only getting clear about what your boundaries are, but being willing to enforce them as well. Enforcing your boundaries may mean ending the relationship if some has unacceptable behaviors and are not willing to change.

The following are some reasonable expectations of a healthy relationship, written as a relationship creed. This is only a sample and it is important that you write your own. Of course, you may use some or all of these expectations and add others as well. If you are doing this work as part of a support group, have other group members sign as witness to your creed. If you are working through this solo have at least one other trusted person sign as a witness. This creates more validity to the creed. The creed maybe framed or at the very least kept in an easily accessible location, such as glued to the inside of your journal. This is to serve as a constant reminder to what your boundaries are.

(SAMPLE) RELATIONSHIP CREED

I, _____, enter into the following agreement with the witness and myself to uphold the following boundaries in my relationships:

I, _____, have a right respect.

I, _____, will not tolerate any form of abuse, whether it is physical, verbal, or otherwise.

I, _____, have a right to express myself without being demeaned.

I, _____, am committed to absolute honesty and I expect nothing less.

I, _____, have a right to be heard.

I, _____, have the right to both a physical and emotionally monogamous relationship.

I, _____, have a right to my own identity.

I, _____, have a right to create sexual boundaries and to have them respected.

I, _____ , have a right to _____

_____

__I, _____ , have a right to_____

_____

____

Signed, Witnessed,

_____   _____

Date: _____   Date: _____

_

Spend a few minutes envisioning your next relationship based on the compatibility exercise and the relationship creed exercise. Describe the characteristics that make up this ideal relationship:

_____

_____

_____

_____

_____

_____

_____

How realistic do you feel it is that you will attain this relationship?

_____

_____

_____

_____

_____

Exercise #51: *Celebrate You!!!*

You have spent your time in the valley, in the dark hour, in the storm, and in the coldest of winter. I know it has been hard and many times you did not think you were going to make it through another night of going to bed with the pain. Many mornings you dreaded going through another day with the heaviness of sadness cloaked about you. But my friend, you have persevered. If you have completed most or all of the healing exercises in this book, you can now see the sun peeking through the clouds and like all storms before this one, the rain is subsiding.

REJOICE!! CELEBRATE!! Yes, you may still feel some sadness or you may have some residual emotions but nothing compared to the first few weeks. It is time to celebrate all you have been through in your season of healing. You have taken your pain and turned it into a journey of self-discovery and self-love. What initially oppressed you has now made you strong. You may not be at the point right now where you are grateful for the pain, but if you continue in this process of healing, you will be grateful if not for the pain for the opportunity to heal.

It is time to CELEBRATE YOU!! Some suggestions for celebrating you are listed below, but whatever you do, do it with **bright colors and in a spirit of celebration!!**

- Wear something bright for seven days

- Buy a bright and colorful picture—hang it up

- Buy some colorful dishes or a multicolored coffee mug

- Dye your hair or get a new hairstyle

- Buy yourself a congratulations card—mail it to yourself

- Buy yourself happy balloons

- Invite close friends (especially those that came to your pity party) to come celebrate with you. Share your accomplishments and the areas of emotional healing and growth with them!

- Share your accomplishments with us at comments@whenrelationshipshurt.com.

Spend at least the next seven days CELEBRATING YOU!!!!

I will do the following each day to celebrate me...

Day 1 _____

_____

_____

Day 2 _____

_____

_____

Day 3 _____

_____

_____

Day 4 _____

_____

_____

Day 5 _____

_____

_____

Day 6 _____

_____

_____

Day 7 _____

_____

_____

Exercise #52: *Stay in the Process*

Life is a process and in order to maintain our healing we must remain in the process. Some suggestions to continue your journey of personal growth and self-love are:

- Attend seminars and workshops dealing with personal growth

- Continue to participate in your support group

- Remain active in your 12-step program

- Continue to journal

- Read self-help/psychology books on relationships, personal growth, and spirituality. I recommend the following books:
  - o *"Are you the one for me"* by Barbara DeAngelis
  - o *"Getting the Love You Want"* by Harville Hendrix
  - o *"In the Meantime"* by Iyanla Vanzant

- Share the information you have learned with others. Help others set up support groups.

- Continue all devotional exercise as you continue to strengthen your personal relationship with God

- List any other activities you will do to maintain your process

_____

_____

_____

_____

_____

_____

I congratulate you and I honor you as you continue on your journey, BE BLESSED!!!

Author's Bio

After a career expanding nearly twenty years, Charlene Sears-Tolbert continues to work passionately as a counselor and educator. She is the CEO and President of WRH Consultants, Inc. Having attended the University of Massachusetts majoring in Human Services Management, Charlene earned a Bachelors degree in Applied Behavioral Science and went on to achieve a Masters degree in Psychology from National Louis University.

Through spiritual practices, a 12-step program, individual counseling, and self-help, Charlene herself, has overcome tremendous obstacles and has made it her life's work to share her experience, strength, and hope to empower others.

Currently, Charlene resides in Orlando, Florida with her son, Shaka Yohance, and her miniature Yorkie, Penelope Ann.

As a gifted and motivated speaker, Charlene is available for workshops, conferences, and retreats. Please contact:

Phone: (407) 367-9876
Fax: (407) 290-5903
Email: Ctolbert@whenrelationshipshurt.com
Write: WRH Consultants, Inc.
          7226 West Colonial Drive, #287
          Orlando, FL 32818

Printed in the United States
By Bookmasters